Welcome dear reader, as we step into the dynamic realm of digital identity, this book serves as your compass, guiding you through the promises and perils that define this ever-evolving landscape.

A thank you,

As I reflect on the journey of writing this book, my heart swells with gratitude for the unwavering support and love of my family, who have been my cornerstone throughout this endeavour. To my loving wife Anita, my partner of 44 remarkable years, your steadfast love and understanding have been my guiding light, making every challenge surmountable and every success sweeter. To Xavier and Didier, my sons, and my daughter-in-law, Sharon, you have been invaluable, continually inspiring me to reach new heights. Your warmth and support have added to the strength that surrounds me.

I am deeply grateful to all those who have contributed to this journey — the mentors who believed in me, colleagues who trusted me, and friends who motivated me. Your collective faith and encouragement have been instrumental in turning the vision of this book into a reality. This book is not just a product of my efforts but a testament to you all. From the bottom of my heart, thank you.

With love and immense gratitude,

Frans Bolk

Foreword

In an era where digital transformation is not just an advantage but a necessity, the European Identity Wallet emerges as a beacon of innovation and security, reshaping the landscape of personal identification and access management. This book is a testament to the relentless pursuit of a connected, secure, and seamless digital Europe—a vision that is now coming to fruition.

At the heart of this book lies the intricate dance of technology with policy, the blend of rigorous security with user-centric design, and the balance of national sovereignty with cross-border interoperability. As you flip through these pages, you will be taken on a journey through the conceptualization, development, and deployment of the European Identity Wallet, an initiative set to revolutionize how citizens and services interact within the digital single market.

The chapters within provide a granular look at the components that make the European Identity Wallet not just a tool, but a gateway to opportunities—facilitating business, streamlining services, and reinforcing the trust of citizens. This book also serves as a guide, detailing a comprehensive project plan for organizations looking to integrate this groundbreaking technology into their operations.

For the buyers of this book, the accompanying project plan stands as a blueprint—a wellspring of knowledge freely available to be tailored to your organization's needs. It is a starting point, a strategic outline designed to be adapted, enriched, and brought to life through your unique vision and execution.

As you embark on this journey, remember that the European Identity Wallet is more than a technological leap; it is a commitment to a future where digital identity empowers, protects, and connects. It is with great anticipation that we look forward to the stories of transformation and success that will emerge as the European Identity Wallet becomes an integral part of our digital lives.

Welcome to the forefront of digital identity.

Sincerely,

Frans Bolk

Founder mob.id

The Growing Need for Digital Identity in Today's World

Identity is intrinsic to human existence...

Let's talk about identity—it's the core of who we are, and now, it's becoming just as crucial online as it is in person. You know how everything seems to be moving to the cloud these days? Well, by 2025, it's predicted that almost all new digital tasks will be happening there. It's a connected world, with online learning becoming a $400 billion arena and telehealth becoming a staple for over 85% of healthcare institutions. But there's a catch: this digital bonanza isn't just a playground for the good guys. It's also a field day for fraudsters, with synthetic identity fraud bleeding the economy of billions each year.

So, what's the game plan? Trust. We've got to establish it digitally. Think about it: banks, hospitals, insurers, and airports—they all need to know you're really you before they let you through the virtual door. But the old ways of proving who we are aren't cutting it anymore. Passwords? They're involved in most data breaches. And physical IDs are easy targets for fakes and frauds.

Now, let's bring in the big guns: regulations. They're like the rulebook for staying in business these days, especially with all the KYC and AML hoops to jump through. Slip up, and the fines can be eye-watering. And don't get me started on GDPR—privacy isn't just nice to have; it's a must-have.

But here's the thing: the legacy systems we've got? They're like trying to fit a square peg in a round hole. Too clunky, too risky, and too old school for our sleek digital world. We're talking about documents that don't translate to bytes and bits, passwords that are more of a headache than a help, and security questions that might as well be public trivia.

So where does that leave us? In need of a makeover for identity management, that's were. We need something that balances security with ease, that keeps our private lives private, and doesn't make us want to pull our hair out every time we log in.

In this chapter, we're going to unpack all this. We'll show you the pitfalls of sticking with the old ways and the perks of switching to smarter, safer digital identities. And we're not just talking theory; we're giving you the real deal, practical solutions that'll work for businesses and regular folks alike. So, let's dive in and figure out how to make our digital selves just as reliable—and recognizable—as our real-world selves. Buckle up; it's going to be an enlightening ride.

Emerging Models of Digital Identity

Let's zoom in on how we're reshaping the identity landscape. Think Self-Sovereign Identity (SSI) as your digital fortress, with you holding the keys to the kingdom. Your personal data stays with you, shared on your terms, through cryptographic exchanges that are as fleeting as they are secure. It's your identity, your rules.

Now, onto Verifiable Credentials—these are like those VIP backstage passes at concerts, but for the digital world. Issued by entities you trust, they're a nod that says you're exactly who you claim to be, allowing for real-time verification without the paper trail.

Then there are Decentralized Identifiers, the digital DNA that's uniquely yours. They're like custom-made name tags that work everywhere you go, independent of any single authority, giving you the freedom to be you across the digital universe.

When anonymity is key, Anonymous Credentials have your back. They're the cryptographic equivalent of a disguise, letting you prove a point without revealing who's behind the mask, ensuring your privacy remains intact.

Biometrics brings your physical uniqueness into the digital domain. Your face, your touch, they're your personal signatures that open doors to a world of convenience and enhanced security.

Imagine your identity seamlessly integrating with your environment—that's the power of IoT and wearables. Your devices recognize you, creating a symphony of smart interactions that make life just a bit easier.

For those times when you're hopping between services, Federated Identity is like having a universal access card. It's a one-time introduction that gives you a smooth ride across various platforms without reiterating your story.

Now, let's address the elephant in the room: blockchain. While it's been hailed as a digital ledger that's tough as nails, it's not the only way to seal the deal on trust. In fact, when it comes to verifying who you are, nothing beats the gold standard of legal identities—like your passport or ID card. These documents are globally recognized and backed by Public Key Infrastructure (PKI) technology, ensuring that trust is built on the solid ground of legal recognition, not just a consensus of unknown parties. Plus, PKI is lightning-fast and reliable, with the kind of trust anchor that blockchain can only aspire to by aggregating validation.

Digital Wallets are the custodians of your digital valuables, organizing and protecting your identity credentials like a high-security vault that's as mobile as you are.

As we weave these technologies into the fabric of our digital lives, we're not just chasing innovation for its own sake. We're building systems rooted in legal legitimacy and augmented by the speed and reliability of PKI. It's about creating a digital identity that's as trustworthy as it is nimble, as private as it is user-friendly. This chapter will guide you through these technologies, showcasing how they empower you to own your identity, ensuring it's recognized and respected everywhere you go—without compromise. Let's build a future where our digital selves are anchored in recognized trust, just as they should be.

Navigating the European Identity Wallet Initiative

In the heart of Europe, a digital revolution is underway. It's called the European Identity Wallet initiative, and it's set to redefine what it means to be digitally you. Born from the 2021 eIDAS regulation, this initiative is not just a tech upgrade; it's a promise to give you—the citizen—a secure handle on your digital identity, no matter where you are in the EU.

Picture this: You choose who holds the keys to your online persona from a roster of trusted organizations. Whether you're booking a train in Rome, seeing a doctor in Berlin, or opening a bank account in Paris, your digital identity follows you, seamless and secure. And it's not just about convenience; it's about control. The initiative is about crafting wallets that not only fit neatly into your digital life but also give you the reins over your personal data. It's privacy, choice, and freedom, all wrapped up in one.

Now, let's get real about what this means on the ground. The initiative is weaving together the best of standards, like the W3C's verifiable credentials, into a tapestry that connects governments and businesses without locking them into one vendor's vision. By mid-2024, the EU's plan is to have these digital wallets certified, recognized, and ready to roll across borders.

But, as with any trailblazing journey, there are mountains to climb. Standardizing this brave new world is tricky. Each tech giant likes to have its walled garden, which doesn't always play nice with others. And while the tech is still finding its feet, there's a bit of a headache in making sure everything clicks together without giving too much power to any one player.

Usability is another puzzle to solve. If your grandma finds it tough to use, then we've missed the mark. We need to make sure that everyone, regardless of age or ability, can step through this new digital door. Plus, we need to educate folks on leaving the cozy, if flawed, world of passwords behind without making them juggle a dozen different wallets.

Legally, it's a bit like the Wild West. Laws are racing to catch up with tech that's sprinting ahead. Different countries have different rules, and in the land of self-sovereign identity, who's to blame when things go south? And with GDPR, we've got to square the circle of keeping records straight while respecting the right to be forgotten.

Then there's the price tag. Setting up the tech can cost a pretty penny, especially for the little guys. Not to mention, finding the brainy tech wizards needed to turn these plans into reality is a quest in itself.

And, of course, we've got to think about society at large. We can't leave anyone behind—every person matters, whether they're tech-savvy or not. Consent can't be a checkbox that's ticked because you feel like you have no choice. And while we're connecting dots and building networks, we've got to ensure we're not accidentally creating a digital Big Brother.

For this digital identity dream to work, it's going to take a village—tech gurus, lawmakers, businesses, and everyday folks. It's about finding that sweet spot where technology serves humanity, not the other way around. So let's roll up our sleeves and get to it. After all, it's not just about shaping an identity system; it's about shaping the future. And that future is looking pretty bright from here.

The European Identity Wallet intends to (EU Toolbox, 2023):

- Give citizens control over their digital identities, attributes, and personal data.
- Prevent identity fraud through use of modern cryptographic protocols.
- Enable citizens to access digital services across EU countries using their national digital identities.
- Provide encapsulated wallets for specific services like banking, healthcare, travel.
- Support anonymous and pseudonymous interactions where appropriate.
- Enable paperless processes and presence-less services through digital identity.
- Foster adoption of privacy-preserving credentials aligned with W3C standards.

The wallet architecture focuses on user ownership, control, and consent for data sharing. By basing the framework on leading standards like W3C verifiable credentials and decentralized identifiers, it aims for vendor-neutral interoperability between government and private systems. The EU intends to establish a certification scheme for European Identity Wallets by mid-2024, enabling cross-border legal recognition and oversight (Europa, 2022).

This initiative exemplifies the potential of rearchitecting digital identity from the ground up around user empowerment. However, transforming such a foundational system also entails surmounting complex challenges at the intersection of technology, ethics, and policy.

Challenges for Adoption of Digital Identity Systems

As we stand on the cusp of a digital identity revolution, we're seeing how emerging models promise a brighter, more secure future. But let's not sugarcoat it—moving away from the old ways is like switching tracks on a speeding train. It's thrilling, sure, but it comes with its fair share of challenges.

First up, standardization—or the lack thereof. It's a bit like everyone speaking different languages in a global conference without a translator. Without universal standards, we're facing a Tower of Babel situation in digital identity. Big tech companies have their own dialects that don't always translate, which stifles the innovation that thrives in open ecosystems. And while we've got some shiny new standards on the block, like DIDs and verifiable credentials, they're still finding their feet, leaving us with a few integration headaches.

Usability is another hurdle. Ever tried juggling too many keys? That's what managing digital keys can feel like, even with the fanciest blockchain tech or credential wallets. And biometrics, while futuristic, aren't always the great equalizer we hope for— imagine not being able to prove who you are because the tech just doesn't recognize you. Plus, we're creatures of habit; teaching people to swap their password post-its for digital wallets won't happen overnight.

Now, let's talk law and order. Regulations are lagging behind like a hiker with a heavy backpack, struggling to keep up with tech sprinting ahead. Different places have different rules, making a unified approach as tough as nailing jelly to a wall. And when things go south, figuring out who's responsible in a self-sovereign world can be as clear as mud. GDPR throws in another curveball—how do you 'forget' something in a ledger that's built to remember?

The cost of all this can make your wallet weep. For smaller organizations, the price of the tech needed can be sky-high, and that's before you even find the tech wizards who can make it all work. And let's not even start on the costs of scaling up— because what's the point of an identity system if it's not for everyone?

But perhaps the biggest challenge is making sure we don't leave anyone behind. Digital identity should be a bridge, not a barrier. It should empower, not exclude. And while we're building this digital world, we've got to ensure we're not accidentally setting up a surveillance state in the process. Balancing privacy with freedom is like walking a tightrope, but it's a walk we need to get right.

To make digital identity systems work for everyone, we need to bring our A-game across technology, governance, law, and society. It's about syncing up our watches and working together to ensure the digital identity landscape is as diverse and inclusive as the people it's designed for. Because at the end of the day, it's not just about connecting dots—it's about connecting lives.

The Promise and Peril of the European Identity Wallet

The European Identity Wallet represents an ambitious undertaking to transform digital identity ecosystems across the European Union. By empowering individuals to control their digital identities, it aims to enhance privacy, security, and user trust. However, an infrastructure transformation of this scale inevitably surfaces complex sociotechnical tensions and trade-offs.

This chapter examines the potential of the European Identity Wallet while unpacking the challenges and uncertainties that must be navigated on the path ahead. We survey the key features and benefits envisioned, while identifying pitfalls that could undermine the constructive vision if not addressed proactively.

Striking the Balance: The European Identity Wallet's Voyage

Let's talk about the European Identity Wallet—Europe's grand plan to revolutionize how we think about and manage digital identities. At its heart, it's about handing the reins of personal data back to the people. The promise? A digital life that's both more private and more secure, where your identity opens doors across the EU with a simple tap.

But when you're changing the game at this level, it's not just about the shiny new tech—it's about the human stories woven through it. We're looking at a seismic shift from big entities holding the keys to you being your own digital gatekeeper. Imagine your digital identity as your most trusted travel companion, one that carries your essentials and presents them only when you say so.

Here's what we're dreaming up:

- **Your data, your rules:** You've got ownership and the power to say who sees what and when.
- **Local is the new global:** Keep your identity data close, stored on your device, not floating in the ether.
- **Sharing with a nod:** Your thumbs-up is needed before your data says hello to the world.
- **Share the need, not the seed:** Transaction-specific info sharing means no oversharing.
- **Your ID, persistent and portable:** Unique IDs like DIDs let you waltz across services without missing a beat.
- **No vendor strings attached:** Universal standards like W3C DIDs mean no lock-ins.
- **Privacy isn't an afterthought:** It's baked right into the architecture.

But, let's not mince words; it's a bit of a tightrope walk. We're trying to thread a needle here—connecting hundreds of systems, kindling user interest across a diverse population, and making sure the tech is as trustworthy as it is cutting-edge. If we don't get it right, we could be looking at early fragmentation, or worse, a digital divide that leaves some stranded on the wrong side of the future.

It's about overcoming the inertia of the old ways—those legacy systems that are as comfortable as an old shoe but nowhere near as nimble as we need. And there's the catch-22: users won't jump on board without useful applications, but developers need an audience to build for. It's a dance of supply and demand, choreographed with precision.

So, what's going to make everyone take the leap? We need those killer apps, the ones that make the case so compelling that everyone from your neighbour to your nan is on board. And let's not forget the institutions, those big ships that don't exactly turn on a dime. They've got to pivot from tried-and-tested to trailblazing, and that's no small feat.

But here's the crux: it's not just about the tech. We're building more than a system; we're building trust. That means diving deep into the ethical quandaries that come with such power. We're painting on a vast canvas, where every stroke affects how freedom, control, and privacy interplay in our lives.

So, we ponder the big questions: how do we prevent a digital "papers please" scenario? How do we ensure this new freedom doesn't become a new form of exclusion? We're on the lookout for those Orwellian pitfalls, ready to steer clear.

The journey ahead is as much about values and vision as it is about verification and validation. We're not just coding a new reality; we're crafting the principles that will define it. This is about building identity ecosystems that bolster, not bulldoze, the pillars of democracy.

With a blend of technology and tenacity, empathy and expertise, we're setting sail towards a horizon where every individual is empowered but not exploited. It's a bold new world, and we're here to make sure it's as inclusive as it is innovative. Let's take the helm together and chart a course for an identity ecosystem that's a beacon of empowerment and equity for all.

Key Capabilities and Benefits

A Journey to Digital Sovereignty

Imagine a wallet, not one tucked in your pocket, but one nestled securely in your phone. This isn't just any wallet; it's the European Identity Wallet, Europe's bold step towards a unified digital identity. Think of it as your digital passport—encrypted, secure, and opening doors across the EU with a simple swipe.

Here's the deal: it's all about giving you a digital identity that's yours to control. You decide what gets shared, when, and with whom. Your personal details? They stay under wraps, shared only with your say-so. It's like having a valet for your virtual valuables, without worrying about prying eyes.

Let's break down what's on offer:

- **A digital vault:** Your identity and credentials are encrypted and stored securely.
- **An anonymous ID card:** Decentralized identifiers keep your private life, well, private.
- **The power of choice:** Share only what's needed for each transaction.
- **The consent conundrum, solved:** You'll give the green light for data sharing.
- **Tailored wallets:** Specialized setups for your banking, healthcare, and travel needs.
- **Universal language:** Interoperability is key, and standards like W3C VC and DIDComm keep everyone on the same page.

The perks? Plenty. Your privacy gets a boost, identity fraud takes a hit, and red tape gets cut. You'll breeze through services across the EU, and the digital single market thrives. It's a win-win.

But let's not gloss over the bumps in the road. We're talking about a seismic shift for a continent's worth of systems, a user base the size of several large countries, and the need to make complex cryptography as palatable as a morning coffee. Scepticism from past tech flops lingers, and the law is always a few steps behind.

Now, imagine trying to change the tires on a moving car. That's what integrating a new digital identity system feels like. It's a colossal task, demanding a shake-up of deep-rooted legacy systems. Users will only hop on board if they see immediate value, and developers need a crowd before they put on a show. We need those early 'aha' moments to spark the movement.

Technologically speaking, we're still in the workshop. The standards are a work in progress, and turning them into something solid and user-friendly is our Herculean task. Meanwhile, institutions big and small are rooted in their ways, and aligning everyone's interests is like herding cats.

Steering clear of Big Brother vibes means building a trust-based ecosystem that respects privacy while fostering transparency. We're not just laying down lines of code; we're laying down the foundations for a trust-based society.

But here's the heart of it: technology must serve humanity, not the other way around. As we navigate this digital transformation, we must ensure that autonomy doesn't come at the expense of accountability, that empowerment doesn't lead to exclusion, and that the drive for innovation doesn't steamroll our civil liberties.

In the pages ahead, we'll explore how to navigate these challenges with grace. We'll look at how to keep the European Identity Wallet from becoming a Pandora's box of digital woes and instead ensure it's a beacon of empowerment, equity, and unity. Join us as we chart a course towards a digital identity that elevates our shared humanity and forges a path of collective empowerment.

Obstacles on the Road to Decentralized Identity

To fulfill its constructive potential, the European Identity Wallet must creatively overcome obstacles including:

Integration Inertia

Redesigning continental-scale identity infrastructure requires integrating countless legacy systems and workflows accumulated over decades. The resulting inertia impedes adopting new decentralized protocols, standards, and models across so many fragmented actors and jurisdictions.

Chicken and Egg Dilemmas

Users won't adopt identity wallets lacking useful applications. But service providers won't build compelling uses cases without critical user mass. Solving this bootstrapping challenge demands strategic coordination between all players.

Needle-Moving Use Cases

Early wins are vital to demonstrate tangible benefits, build confidence, and light the way. But which high-impact use cases could catalyse adoption? The killer apps for decentralized identity remain elusive.

Technological Maturity

Core standards like DIDComm messaging and verifiable credentials remain unstable, hindering development. Migrating from specs to production-grade implementations is the perennial challenge.

Institutional Inertia

Transitioning from legacy identity systems requires overcoming tremendous institutional inertia across both public and private sector organizations. Their existing workflows, processes, and systems resist disruptive paradigm shifts, regardless of technical merits.

Lack of Incentive Alignment

Without shared vision and incentives, key players often sub-optimize from their narrow vantagepoints. But coordinating ecosystems requires aligning Stakeholders around value propositions.

Uncertainty Avoidance

Breaking from the familiar status quo requires risk tolerance. But the uncertainty of decentralization breeds hesitance in change-averse established institutions.

Lack of Boundary Resources

Successful ecosystems depend on boundary resources like shared data models, APIs, standards, and policies. But few such assets exist currently to connect ecosystem actors.

Overcoming these barriers demands acknowledging difficulties, adapting intelligently, and laying the social foundation for trust-based ecosystems. Both technology and people must evolve in tandem.

Towards an Ethical Compass

As with any transformative technology, we must also examine the European digital identity wallet through an ethical lens balancing empowerment and accountability.

While expanding individual control over digital identities fosters autonomy, how do we balance oversight for social welfare? If decentralized architectures remove central points of control, how to uphold responsibility? Does "code is law" erode civil liberties that evolved over centuries?

And if identity underlays access to livelihoods, finances and mobility, how do we ensure solutions don't exacerbate exclusion? Could we unintentionally recreate "papers please" societies where identity determines basic opportunity? Does a "wallet score" emerge mirroring China's social credit system?

These questions have no easy answers. But grappling with ethical tensions will shape whether decentralized identity uplifts or corrupts. The solutions we choose reflect the future we envision.

While technology provides tools, we must guide their use towards human dignity, equity and justice. Only by recognizing this higher purpose can we build identity ecosystems as nourishers of democracy rather than destroyers.

With empathy and wisdom, we can yet chart a course that benefits all through empowerment, not exploitation.

Trust

The Fabric of Trust — Weaving Identity with Assurance in the European Identity Wallet

Introduction: Trust in Digital Identity In the digital age, trust is the cornerstone upon which the edifice of online interaction is built. The European Identity Wallet is a testament to this philosophy, intertwining advanced technology with the golden thread of trust. Within this chapter, we'll unravel the factors that constitute the trust of an identity—trust anchors, biometry, and biographical attributes—and illuminate how the European Identity Wallet is the embodiment of these principles.

The Trust Anchor: Foundation of Assurance A trust anchor represents the cornerstone of digital security—a reference point from which all validation checks are derived. In the context of identity, a trust anchor could be a state-certified digital signature, ensuring that the identity is recognized and can be unequivocally trusted. The European Identity Wallet is rooted in such trust anchors, providing a state-backed assurance that an individual's digital identity is authentic and verifiable.

Biometry: The Personal Stroke of Trust Biometry introduces a personal layer to trust. By using unique biological traits for verification, such as fingerprints or facial recognition, biometry ensures that the individual claiming an identity is indeed who they purport to be. The European Identity Wallet leverages biometric verification, tying the physical uniqueness of an individual to their digital identity, thus providing a robust, personal trust factor that is difficult to replicate or forge.

Biographical Attributes: The Narrative of Trust Biographical attributes are the details that form the narrative of an individual's identity—name, date of birth, nationality, etc. These attributes, when verified against trusted sources like civil registries, enhance the trust quotient of an individual's identity. The European Identity Wallet incorporates these attributes, ensuring they are accurately captured and securely stored within the wallet, ready for verification when needed.

Integration of Trust Factors in the European Identity Wallet

The European Identity Wallet is a harmonious blend of these trust factors:

- **Trust Anchor Integration:** The wallet's architecture is intrinsically linked to state-verified trust anchors, ensuring that the identities it holds are anchored in a foundation of trust.
- **Biometric Assurance:** By incorporating biometric elements, the wallet offers a seamless yet secure mode of identity verification that is both user-friendly and exceptionally reliable.
- **Incorporation of Biographical Data:** The wallet includes essential biographical attributes that provide a complete and verified identity profile, making it a comprehensive tool for both citizens and authorities.

Challenges and Considerations While the wallet's design is sophisticated, the road to widespread adoption involves navigating challenges such as ensuring user privacy, interoperability with various systems, and the integration of emerging technologies without disrupting existing infrastructures.

The Road Ahead for Trust and Identity Trust, when woven into the fabric of digital identity, can transform how we interact, transact, and establish our presence in the digital realm. The European Identity Wallet, with its robust trust architecture, stands as a beacon of this transformation, paving the way towards a future where digital identity is synonymous with security, privacy, and reliability. As we look ahead, the wallet is not just a tool but a journey towards a more trusted digital Europe.

When considering the implementation and use of any digital system, it's important to recognize that while there are inherent risks, these should not deter us from leveraging its benefits. Instead, they serve as a reminder of the need for caution and the importance of implementing appropriate measures. Identifying potential risks early on allows for the development of effective strategies to mitigate them. This proactive approach ensures that while we harness the advantages of the system, we also safeguard against potential vulnerabilities, maintaining a balance between innovation and security. Thus, acknowledging these risks is not a sign of weakness, but rather a step towards responsible and resilient usage

Inside the European Identity Wallet
Architectures, Protocols and Technologies

In the vibrant digital tapestry of Europe, where every thread represents a unique identity, the European Identity Wallet emerges as a pivotal innovation. It's a bold stride towards harmonizing our digital interactions, crafted with the promise of bolstering security and fostering seamless connections across borders. This initiative isn't just a concept; it's the manifestation of a collective vision for a connected future, built upon the bedrock of trust and user empowerment. While the aspirations of the European Identity Wallet are far-reaching, realizing this vision depends on pragmatic technological building blocks. This chapter dives into the key architectures, protocols and technologies powering decentralized identity wallets.

Let's embark on an exploratory journey through the architectural wonders, the protocols that guide our digital pathways, and the technologies that are the lifeblood of the decentralized identity wallets. We're not just talking about established pillars like Public Key Infrastructure (PKI), which has long been the guardian of our digital interactions. We're also venturing into the realm of breakthroughs, where verifiable credentials and blockchain identities are the new frontiers. Understanding these pillars is key to unlocking the potential of next-gen identity systems.

Public Key Infrastructure

Public Key Infrastructure is the stalwart of digital trust, a system where digital certificates and cryptographic keys come together to secure our digital identities. Imagine a world where every identity has a matching pair of keys:

- **The Public Key:** A digital open door, inviting secure communications from anyone who knocks.

- **The Private Key:** The secret keyholder, ensuring that messages are only read by the intended eyes.

Public key infrastructure (PKI) provides the basis for securely managing digital identities and enabling trust online. PKI uses digital certificates and public key cryptography to establish identity and enable trusted information exchange.

Certificates are the golden seals of trust, linking an entity's identity to their public key through the validation of a trusted Certificate Authority (CA). These certificates are the cornerstones of our digital interactions, enabling:

- Secure conversations shielded from eavesdropping.
- Digital signatures that seal authenticity and integrity.
- Trustworthy verification of identities in the vast digital landscape.

PKI is the foundation of our trusted digital ecosystem, a pivotal element in the identity wallet infrastructure that issues certificates to individuals and organizations alike. It's the invisible sentinel that guards our digital exchanges, ensuring that the right keys open the right doors.

PKI is thus essential for trusted digital environments.

The identity wallet ecosystem leverages PKI by having approved certificate authorities issue identity certificates to individuals and organizations. PKI provides the basis for trusted digital identity ecosystems using public-private key pairs, digital certificates, and cryptographic operations.

Key components include:

- Certificate Authority - Validates identities and issues digital certificates
- Registration Authority - Verifies identity documents and processes certificate requests
- Public Key - Shared openly to allow encryption
- Private Key - Secret key to decrypt messages
- Digital Certificates - Bind identities to their public key

Key PKI standards:

- X.509 - Defines certificate format
- PKCS - Public-key cryptography standards
- CPS - Certification practice statement

PKI allows:

- **Encryption** - Scramble messages that only recipient can decrypt
- **Signing** - Bind identities to documents using private keys
- **Authentication** - Match public keys to established identities

PKI is critical for secure communications and transactions. But centralized authorities create single points of failure.

Decentralized Identifiers (DIDs)

Now, let's talk about the decentralized evolution of identity—Decentralized Identifiers (DIDs). Imagine shaking off the shackles of centralized systems where identities are scattered across various domains. DIDs present a unified solution: persistent and globally unique identifiers that aren't beholden to any central authority. They're the new passports in the digital realm, containing public keys and other critical information, all while ensuring that you remain the master of your digital self.

DIDs are the bedrock upon which user-centric identity wallets are built. They enable you to carry your digital credentials, unfettered by platforms or providers, ensuring your identity is recognized across the EU's digital expanse. For the EU identity wallet to truly thrive, these DIDs must be compliant and registered under the EU's trusted eIDAS framework—this is non-negotiable.

As we traverse this new digital identity landscape, the European Identity Wallet stands as a bastion of innovation, a tool for unity, and a harbinger of a secure, integrated digital Europe. Through this book, we invite you to join us on this journey, to embrace the new horizons of identity, and to weave your thread into the digital tapestry of Europe.

A challenge with traditional PKI is identities get fragmented across different certificate authorities and namespaces. Decentralized identifiers (DIDs) offer a solution by creating persistent, globally unique identifiers not tied to central authorities.

DIDs comprise URI-based identifiers like:

did:example:abcdef123456789

Along with DID documents containing metadata like public keys, service endpoints, verification methods, timestamps, and signatures.

DIDs allow creating verifiable, portable digital identities owned and controlled by users. The W3C DID specification enables interoperability between different DID methods from Microsoft, Sovrin, and others.

DIDs are foundational for user-centric identity wallets. They detached identities from centralized providers and anchor digital relationships. The EU identity wallet requires compliant DID methods be registered in the EU Trusted List of eIDAS to ensure legal validity.

DIDs create globally unique, persistent identifiers independent of authorities.

Key Properties:

- Self-ownership - Users fully control their DID
- Persistence - DIDs remain stable over time
- Global uniqueness - No collisions between DIDs
- Cryptography - DIDs verifiable via public keys
- Portability - DIDs operate across any system
- Privacy - DIDs minimize personal data exposure

DIDs comprise:

- URI - Unique identifier like did:example:123456
- DID Document - Metadata like public keys and service endpoints
- DID Methods - Specific DID implementations

DIDs enable interoperable digital identity not tied to isolated namespaces. The W3C DID standard ensures portability between different DID methods.

DIDs form the backbone for user-centric identity. EU identity wallets require compliant DID methods registered under eIDAS.

Verifiable Credentials

While DIDs offer decentralized identifiers, verifiable credentials enable exchanging validated identity claims.

Verifiable credentials (VCs) are digitally signed assertions containing identity attributes packaged in cryptographic containers. For example:

```
{

  "name": "John Smith",

    "dateOfBirth": "1980-01-01",

    "credentials": {...}

}
```

The credentials payload has issuer signature(s) to make it tamper-evident and verifiable.

Holders can selectively disclose VCs to share validated identity claims without exposing raw personal data. This preserves privacy far better than physical documents like passports.

VCs align with the info card identity metasystem pattern promoted by Kim Cameron and others to package identity data as claims rather than cumbersome identities. The EU identity wallet will leverage VCs based on the emerging W3C standard.

Verifiable credentials enable exchanging validated identity claims.

Key properties:

- Tamper-evident - Digitally signed to detect alterations
- Machine-verifiable - Claims authenticated programmatically
- Selective disclosure - Only required claims revealed
- Privacy-preserving - Avoid raw personal data sharing
- Revocable - Credentials can be revoked by issuer
- Non-correlatable - Issued pseudo-anonymously

VCs comprise:

- Claims - Identity attributes e.g., name, age, degree
- Proofs - Signatures to verify authenticity
- Metadata - Issuance details like expiry and revocation status

VCs align with the info card identity metasystem pattern to package identity data as verifiable claims rather than cumbersome entire identities.

The EU Identity Wallet will leverage W3C Verifiable Credentials to share validated attributes.

Identity Hubs

To exchange verifiable credentials while preserving user privacy, identity hubs allow secure communication without a common ledger.

Identity hubs serve as blind intermediaries that:

- Enable credential issuers and verifiers to coordinate without sharing ledgers.
- Avoid revealing transaction metadata that could compromise user privacy.
- Provide discovery services to look up entities to transact with.

Hubs reference identifiers like DIDs and route selectively shared credentials using encrypted channels, facilitating coordination while limiting data exposure.

The peer DIDComm protocol extends this with end-to-end encrypted messaging between hubs to share credentials and proofs. Hubs will likely form a key integration layer for the EU identity wallet ecosystem.

Identity Wallets

At the user level, identity wallets serve as applications to manage digital identifiers, credentials, keys, and other identity attributes. Leading standards include the FIDO credential management API and the Decentralized Key Management System (DKMS).

Wallets allow users to:

- Securely store critical identity documents—think of eIDs, driver's licenses, and passports—as personal treasures locked away in a digital vault.
- Manage a medley of keys and credentials spanning across various identity providers, much like a seasoned conductor leading an orchestra of access points.
- Engage in the art of selective disclosure, crafting zero-knowledge proofs that share only the essential, never more.

- Navigate trusted data exchanges with deliberate consent, placing the power of 'yes' or 'no' firmly in the user's hands.
- Maintain a continuous thread of identity across services and contexts, ensuring one's digital self remains intact and consistent

By encapsulating identity capabilities, wallets enhance user control, privacy and convenience. Both platform-provided and standalone wallet applications will be integral to adoption.

Identity hubs route verifiable credentials while limiting exposure.

Capabilities:

- Secure routing - Privacy-preserving exchange of credentials
- Selective disclosure - Only share required claims
- Blind intermediaries - Don't retain transaction metadata
- Discovery services - Lookup entities to transact with
- End-to-end encryption - Protect data in transit

Hubs help coordinate credential issuers and verifiers without a shared ledger. Communication occurs via protocols like DIDComm.

Hubs will enable integration between identity wallet providers, government agencies, and other ecosystem entities.

Identity wallets manage user identifiers, keys, credentials, proofs, etc.

Enveloping these capabilities, identity wallets are not just functional—they're an enhancement of user autonomy, privacy, and convenience. Whether provided as part of a platform or standing alone as an app, these wallets are critical to fostering widespread adoption of digital identities.

Features:

- Encrypted storage - For identity documents, keys and credentials
- Credential management - Organize claims from different providers
- Selective disclosure - Reveal only necessary data
- Consent mechanisms - Control over data sharing
- Continuity - Persistence of identity across services
- Backup and recovery - For disaster resilience

Leading standards include FIDO credential management API and DKMS.

Wallets enhance user control, privacy and convenience when using digital identity.

As we traverse this landscape, identity hubs stand as sentinels of secure routing, champions of privacy. They enable a world where the exchange of credentials occurs without unwarranted disclosure, where discovery services act as guides in a vast digital ecosystem, and where end-to-end encryption is the guardian of our data in transit.

Together, hubs and wallets are the dual pillars supporting a future where managing digital identity becomes second nature—intuitive, secure, and unobtrusive. They are not just tools but enablers of a digital Europe that respects the sanctity of personal data while heralding an era of effortless and protected digital interaction.

Blockchain Identity

While not required, blockchain offers intriguing capabilities for decentralized identity systems regarding verifiability, persistence and accountability.

By encoding identity transactions on a tamper-proof shared ledger, blockchains can provide:

- Immutable proof of identity events like key issuance, credential validation, and authorization.
- Censorship resistance by distributing identity data across nodes.
- Cryptographic validation of historical identity transactions.
- Automated interactions via smart contract rules.

However, downsides like poor scalability, high cost, and ecological impact pose adoption challenges. Selective use cases requiring irrefutable records like contracts may justify blockchain integration.

While optional, blockchain provides unique capabilities.

Benefits:

- Persistence - Identities exist long-term on blockchain
- Auditability - Transactions immutably recorded
- Verifiability - Cryptography proves identity events
- Availability - Distributed ledgers avoid single points of failure
- Automation - Smart contracts execute identity workflows

But issues like scalability, cost, and environmental impact require consideration. Select applications like contracts warrant blockchains.

PKI-Based Identity: The Keystone of Digital Trust

In the pursuit of a resilient digital identity framework, the PKI-based identity stands out, not as an alternative, but as the bedrock of trust and verification. Here, the trust anchor is not a distributed ledger but the solid ground of a state-backed electronic signature. This signature, a PKI-based electronic marvel, carries the weight of authenticity, integrity, and validity, and it does so without the need for blockchain's validation.

The PKI-based identity carries its trust within, a fortress of verification where the state's electronic signature acts as an unassailable seal of legitimacy. Each PKI identity is a testament to:

- An unbreakable chain of trust, with every key issuance, credential validation, and authorization anchored in the state's electronic signature.
- The resilience of a system where data doesn't just reside on disparate nodes but is bound to the identity itself, verified and recognized across borders and domains.
- A history of interactions, not recorded on a blockchain, but inscribed in the cryptographic layers of the identity, each transaction a brushstroke of the user's digital journey.
- The fluidity of interactions, governed not by smart contracts, but by the robust rules and standards set forth by certifying authorities, ensuring that workflows remain seamless and secure.

This PKI-based ecosystem transcends the need for blockchain's indelible record-keeping by embedding trust directly into the identity. It's a system that is inherently scalable, cost-efficient, and eco-conscious, circumventing the challenges often faced by blockchain implementations.

Benefits of the PKI-based identity include:

- **Enduring Trust:** Identities are intrinsically secure, backed by the immutable confidence of state-sanctioned electronic signatures.

- **Inherent Auditability:** Every credential and key is an open book to those with the right to read it, with the state's signature as the table of contents.
- **Seamless Verifiability:** The state's electronic signature provides a reliable compass for navigating the validity of each identity, no blockchain needed.
- **Unwavering Availability:** Reliance on a centralized, authoritative trust anchor means identities are not subject to the whims of distributed ledger technologies.
- **Effortless Integration:** PKI-based identities integrate into existing workflows with ease, reducing the need for extensive system overhauls.

In scenarios where the indomitable assurance of identity is paramount, the PKI-based identity shines, free from the constraints and considerations that blockchain carries. It's a system where the identity doesn't just speak for itself—it speaks with the authority of the state, and it speaks volumes.

Holistic Foundations

Technical architectures provide a starting point but holistic frameworks are needed to guide development. The Pan-Canadian Trust Framework offers an exemplar with its governance model spanning legal, business, semantic, and technical layers. Europe must similarly evolve multi-layer frameworks, not just technologies.

Technical foundations enable next-generation identity but holistic frameworks are essential for adoption. The Pan-Canadian Trust Framework exemplifies governing identity across legal, business, semantic and technical layers.

Europe similarly needs multi-layer governance spanning policy, economics, sociology, data, and technology. With wisdom and diligence, technical capabilities can unlock more equitable and empowering social systems. But the road ahead remains arduous.

The path forward entails patiently laying technological and human foundations while navigating complex systemic interactions and unintended consequences. But with diligence and wisdom, decentralized identity offers a historic opportunity to reshape society for the better.

Trust in Digital Identity

In the digital age, trust is the cornerstone upon which the edifice of online interaction is built. The European Identity Wallet is a testament to this philosophy, intertwining advanced technology with the golden thread of trust. Within this chapter, we'll unravel the factors that constitute the trust of an identity—trust anchors, biometry, and biographical attributes—and illuminate how the European Identity Wallet is the embodiment of these principles.

- **The Trust Anchor:** Foundation of Assurance A trust anchor represents the cornerstone of digital security—a reference point from which all validation checks are derived. In the context of identity, a trust anchor could be a state-certified digital signature, ensuring that the identity is recognized and can be unequivocally trusted. The European Identity Wallet is rooted in such trust anchors, providing a state-backed assurance that an individual's digital identity is authentic and verifiable.

- **Biometry:** The Personal Stroke of Trust Biometry introduces a personal layer to trust. By using unique biological traits for verification, such as fingerprints or facial recognition, biometry ensures that the individual claiming an identity is indeed who they purport to be. The European Identity Wallet leverages biometric verification, tying the physical uniqueness of an individual to their digital identity, thus providing a robust, personal trust factor that is difficult to replicate or forge.

- **Biographical Attributes:** The Narrative of Trust Biographical attributes are the details that form the narrative of an individual's identity—name, date of birth, nationality, etc. These attributes, when verified against trusted sources like civil registries, enhance the trust quotient of an individual's identity. The European Identity Wallet incorporates these attributes, ensuring they are accurately captured and securely stored within the wallet, ready for verification when needed.

Integration of Trust Factors in the European Identity Wallet

The European Identity Wallet is a harmonious blend of these trust factors:

- **Trust Anchor Integration:** The wallet's architecture is intrinsically linked to state-verified trust anchors, ensuring that the identities it holds are anchored in a foundation of trust.
- **Biometric Assurance:** By incorporating biometric elements, the wallet offers a seamless yet secure mode of identity verification that is both user-friendly and exceptionally reliable.

- **Incorporation of Biographical Data:** The wallet includes essential biographical attributes that provide a complete and verified identity profile, making it a comprehensive tool for both citizens and authorities.

Challenges and Considerations While the wallet's design is sophisticated, the road to widespread adoption involves navigating challenges such as ensuring user privacy, interoperability with various systems, and the integration of emerging technologies without disrupting existing infrastructures.

The Road Ahead for Trust and Identity

Trust, when woven into the fabric of digital identity, can transform how we interact, transact, and establish our presence in the digital realm. The European Identity Wallet, with its

robust trust architecture, stands as a beacon of this transformation, paving the way towards a future where digital identity is synonymous with security, privacy, and reliability. As we look ahead, the wallet is not just a tool but a journey towards a more trusted digital Europe.

European Identity Wallet Applications and Use Cases

While the European Identity Wallet aims to provide a universal digital identity platform for the region, its potential value must be demonstrated through tangible use cases. This chapter explores key applications that could benefit from decentralized identity wallets, along with examples of how they might work in practice. We also examine limitations and concerns that must be addressed even with compelling use cases.

Travel and Hospitality

In the ever-evolving sphere of travel and hospitality, the digital wallet emerges not just as a convenience but as a revolution in the passenger experience. It heralds a new chapter where journeys are less about the paperwork and more about the adventure itself

Imagine a world where your passport, visa, and boarding passes are no longer physical entities but secure digital companions within your wallet:

- Effortlessly present your travel credentials to airlines and hotels, transforming verification into a simple tap on your screen.
- Navigate check-ins, immigration, and boarding with a swiftness that turns these processes into mere formalities.
- Glide from the airport terminal to your rental car, and into your hotel room with nothing but your mobile wallet—elegant, secure, and keycard-free.

The promise of this digital transformation is immense, yet it carries the weight of responsibility—to ensure that the tapestry of travellers, regardless of their affinity for technology, is not frayed by progress. It's a pursuit where inclusivity must be the co-pilot, guiding us to a destination where convenience is universal.

The quantifiable benefits of adopting digital wallets in travel are significant:

- **Elevated Passenger Experiences:** The reduction of queues and the simplification of identity checks carve out more time for leisure and less for logistics. Surveys indicate that the hassle of identity verification often casts a shadow over travel joy.
- **Operational Efficiency:** The ripple effect of wallets extends to airlines and hotels, where the automation of identity checks translates into reduced overheads. Studies suggest that European airports alone could witness savings in the hundreds of millions. One estimate found €160 million in savings for airports in Europe.
- **Fortified Security:** Digital wallets are bastions against identity theft, with biometric credentials acting as stalwart guardians. The alarming rates of fraud in travel loyalty programs underscore the necessity of robust security measures. 21% of travel loyalty program members experience fraud annually
- **Innovation in Services:** The integration of value-added services within wallets—like exclusive offers, real-time luggage tracking, and seamless car rentals—paints a future where the wallet is not just a tool but an experience enhancer.

Travel as a promising use case for digital wallets can simplify verification and enhance the passenger experience. Features include:

- Securely store passport, visa, and other travel credentials on wallet
- Use verifiable credentials to validate credentials with airlines, hotels etc.
- Streamline check-in, immigration and boarding without physical documents
- More seamless car rental pick-up and drop-off using digital licenses
- Access hotel rooms via mobile wallet instead of plastic keycards

While promising, risks around excluding less tech-savvy groups must be mitigated. Usability for diverse populations is essential.

Here are some statistics on the potential advantages and impacts of using electronic identities for air travellers:

- According to the International Air Transport Association (IATA), using electronic IDs could reduce passenger check-in times by 2.5 minutes per flight. For airports with 40 million passengers per year, this could result in savings of €200 million annually.
- IATA estimates that automating passport checks using ePassports could reduce waiting times at immigration by up to 30%. This could help airports accommodate increased passenger volumes more efficiently.
- A survey by SITA found that 73% of air travellers are interested in using a digital ID on their smartphones for airport processes instead of paper IDs and boarding passes. This highlights the demand for digital convenience.
- In a trial by AirAsia, the use of digital IDs to verify passenger identities before airport arrival reduced the average check-in and bag drop time from 12 minutes to under 1 minute.

- Heathrow Airport's biometric boarding trials found that using electronic passports and facial recognition could reduce the average boarding gate processing time from 12 minutes to 2.5 minutes per flight.
- Accenture estimates that 100% adoption of biometric boarding using ePassports could eliminate over 240 million paper boarding passes annually, saving the air transport industry $2.1 billion per year.

So, in summary, key advantages of using electronic IDs in air travel include faster processing times, cost savings for airports, increased passenger satisfaction, and environmental benefits from reducing paper waste. The statistics highlight the substantial efficiency gains and customer experience improvements possible.

The potential revenue streams from digital wallet adoption in travel are as varied as they are lucrative:

- Subscription fees for wallet services, ensuring uninterrupted premium experiences.
- Value-added features that cater to the discerning traveller seeking that extra layer of convenience or luxury.
- Commissions harvested from bookings and transactions facilitated by the wallet's ecosystem.
- Advertising tailored to the traveller's context and preferences, turning the wallet into a marketplace of opportunities.
- The sale of anonymized analytics, offering insights into traveller behaviours and trends.

The digital wallet in travel and hospitality is more than an innovation; it's the beginning of a journey towards a seamless, secure, and more enjoyable travel experience. As we embark on this path, let's navigate the skies and lands with a spirit of inclusivity, paving the way for every traveller to explore the world with ease and assurance.

Healthcare

In the labyrinthine world of healthcare, where well-being meets bureaucracy, digital health wallets stand as beacons of transformation. These digital guardians promise a future where medical credentials and records are no longer static notes in a file but dynamic, secure elements that patients and providers can access with a touch or a click.

Envision a healthcare landscape where:

- Patients are the custodians of their medical narratives, wielding the power to grant access to their history, diagnostic tests, and prescriptions.
- Healthcare professionals authenticate their credentials swiftly, stepping into their roles with the certainty that access privileges are up to date.
- The exchange of records between insurers, pharmacies, and care providers becomes a secure, seamless symphony of information sharing.
- Claims for insurance and pharmacy pickups are substantiated with ease, devoid of the usual rigmarole of proof and paperwork.
- Medical data, anonymized to the core, becomes a wellspring of insights for researchers, all while holding the sanctity of patient privacy inviolate.

Yet, the path to this utopia is not without its hurdles. The intricate web of healthcare ecosystems, bound by rigorous regulations, demands not just adoption but adaptation. Coordinated efforts among stakeholders are not just desirable—they are indispensable.

The integration of identity wallets into healthcare heralds a plethora of advantages:

- **Elevated Patient Care:** The immediacy of medical history access equips providers with a holistic view, enabling informed decisions at the bedside or in the operating room.
- **Cost Efficiency:** Projections show staggering potential savings—up to 30%—by cutting through the red tape of duplicative procedures and the maze of paperwork.
- **User Empowerment:** Patients navigate their healthcare journey with newfound autonomy, no longer burdened by the repetitive task of recounting their medical history.
- **Robust Security:** These digital vaults of health information bolster defences against the spectre of falsification and the breach of sensitive data.

Public Health Advancements: Anonymized datasets become the lifeblood of medical research and the compass for informed policymaking.

Wallets could securely manage medical credentials and records to improve healthcare:

- Patients control access to medical history, tests, prescriptions etc.
- Professionals verify credentials to confirm licenses and access privileges
- Securely share records between insurers, pharmacies and care providers
- Prove eligibility for insurance claims or pharmacy pickups
- Anonymize data for research while preserving privacy

But complex ecosystems and stringent regulations pose adoption challenges. Stakeholder coordination is critical.

Advantages of identity wallets in healthcare:

- Improved patient care - Instant access to medical histories helps providers make informed treatment decisions.
- Lower costs - Up to 30% savings estimated in the US by eliminating duplicative tests and paperwork.
- Better user experience - Patients avoid repeatedly providing info and can securely access records anywhere.
- Enhanced security - Guard against record falsification and unauthorized access to sensitive info.
- Public health gains - Anonymized data aids medical research and policymaking.

Here are some statistics on the potential benefits of using electronic identities and health records in healthcare:

- According to a study by McKinsey, the use of digital health records could reduce duplicate testing and administrative costs by up to 30% in the United States, representing over $190 billion in annual savings.
- The EU estimates that electronic health records exchanged between healthcare providers could generate savings of €5.4 billion per year in the European Union.
- 90% of physicians believe that electronic health records improve overall patient care quality by enhancing access to patient data.
- A Mayo Clinic study found that use of electronic medical records reduces the likelihood of medication errors by 55-86%.

- During a 4-month trial, Geisinger Health System's use of digital health records was associated with a 20% decrease in hospital admissions.
- Patient wait times at facilities using digital health records decreased by approximately 35%, according to various studies.
- A study found that electronic prescribing through digital health records can reduce the number of adverse drug events by nearly 50% compared to paper-based prescribing.
- Digital transfer of prescriptions instead of paper scripts could save the US healthcare system $27 billion annually based on a study by Surescripts.

In summary, transitioning to digital identities and health records provides substantial benefits in terms of reduced costs, improved patient care, greater efficiency, and fewer medical errors. The statistics make a compelling case for accelerating their adoption across the healthcare industry.

As for the economic architecture underpinning digital health wallets, the models are as innovative as they are diverse:

- Healthcare organizations can adopt wallet platforms, ushering in an era of digital efficiency.
- Credential management and verification APIs present licensing opportunities that promise to streamline operations.
- Data exchanges can generate transaction fees, fostering a self-sustaining ecosystem of information sharing.
- Identity providers might explore subscription models, ensuring continuity and security of service.
- Research endeavours can be propelled forward with grants, rewarding the exploration of health data for groundbreaking insights.

Digital health wallets are not simply a technological advancement; they are a paradigm shift in healthcare management. They offer a vision of a world where healthcare is more accessible, secure, and tailored to individual needs— where the journey to health is a partnership paved with trust and fortified by the assurance of digital innovation.

Revenue models:

- Selling wallet platforms to healthcare organizations
- Licensing credential management and verification APIs
- Transaction fees for data exchange
- Subscriptions for identity providers
- Grants for novel research based on health data insights

Finance

Finance Reimagined: The Integration of Identity Wallets

The financial sector, a cornerstone of global commerce and personal prosperity, stands on the cusp of a revolution with the introduction of identity wallets. These digital conduits of identity verification promise to streamline the world of finance, from Know Your Customer (KYC) protocols to the day-to-day management of assets.

Envision a financial ecosystem where:

- The KYC process becomes a streamlined affair, minimizing data exposure while maximizing efficiency.
- Accounts, cards, and even the burgeoning realm of crypto wallets are managed with fortified security under the user's watchful eye.
- Contactless payments are executed with a mere wave of a mobile wallet, transforming transactions into a seamless dance of digital exchange.

- The spectres of identity theft and unauthorized account access are held at bay through layers of cryptographic defence.

Yet, integrating this new wave of technology with the stalwart legacy systems of banking is not without its challenges. The path forward requires a delicate balance of enhancing usability without compromising the bedrock of security.

The adoption of identity wallets in finance carries a treasure trove of advantages:

- **Enhanced Customer Onboarding:** The friction of traditional application processes fades, with abandonment rates plummeting as digital ID verification becomes instantaneous.
- **Cost Reductions:** The shift to digital onboarding translates into tangible savings, trimming the financial outlays required for welcoming each new customer.
- **Fortified Defences:** Cutting-edge biometrics and cryptography create a bulwark against fraud, safeguarding institutions from the financial haemorrhage caused by account takeovers.
- **Innovative Services:** The integration of digital loyalty programs with wallets invites a new paradigm of personalized services and streamlined payments.
- **Regulatory Compliance:** Adherence to KYC and anti-money laundering (AML) regulations is streamlined, averting the risk of punitive fines.

Here are some statistics on the potential benefits of using digital identities and records in the finance sector:

- Accenture estimates that digital identity verification could save banks over $20 billion annually in KYC (know your customer) and customer onboarding costs.

- The use of digital signatures for account opening and loan processing can reduce turnaround time by over 80% compared to paper-based manual workflows, per a study by Deloitte.
- Shared digital KYC processes enabled by electronic IDs could reduce KYC processing costs for banks by 60-70%, according to a report by McKinsey.
- Electronic IDs could enable over 1 billion new people globally to access financial services by addressing issues like lack of paperwork, McKinsey projects.
- Digital IDs could unlock an estimated 72 million new bank accounts, leading to approximately $250 billion in incremental deposits for banks, per McKinsey estimates.
- Fintech applications based on digital identities could add over $250 billion in loans across emerging economies.
- The use of digital channels and electronic signatures increased European consumer lending volumes by 3-4x compared to paper-based processes, according to Capgemini.
- 90% of bank customers said they would prefer using digital identity apps vs physically visiting branches, according to an HSBC survey.
- Increased onboarding conversion - Application abandonment drops over 40% with instant digital ID verification.
- Lower costs - $3-4 saving per new digital bank customer versus physical onboarding.
- Improved security - Biometrics and cryptography limit fraud like account takeovers which cost US banks $5 billion annually.
- New offerings - Digital loyalty programs integrated with payments and personalized services.

- Compliance - Adhering to KYC and AML regulations to avoid major fines.

In summary, digital IDs and electronic signatures can substantially streamline processes and reduce costs for financial institutions while increasing consumer access and convenience. The statistics highlight the transformative potential of secure, verified digital identity management in the finance industry.

In the realm of revenue, identity wallets in finance open up diverse streams:

- **Transaction Fees:** Each digital transaction can contribute a small fee, supporting the maintenance and growth of the wallet ecosystem.
- **Product Commissions:** Financial products recommended or facilitated through the wallet can yield commissions, creating mutual benefits for users and providers.
- **Premium Features:** Subscriptions and add-ons cater to the discerning consumer, offering advanced features for those seeking a tailored financial management experience.
- **Data-Driven Insights:** The analytical power harnessed from transaction data can inform lending risk models and drive business intelligence.
- **Targeted Advertising:** Wallet apps can host advertising, transforming them into platforms for financial product discovery and promotion.

The introduction of identity wallets into the finance sector is not just an upgrade—it's a reimagination of financial interaction, offering a future where managing finances is not only secure but also a delightfully streamlined aspect of everyday life.

e-Government

In the domain of public services, where bureaucracy often weaves a complex tapestry, digital wallets emerge as streamlined portals to civic engagement. These wallets are not merely tools but catalysts for a more engaged and efficient relationship between citizens and government.

Imagine a society where:

- Proving eligibility for government benefits is a matter of digital simplicity, ensuring that support reaches those who need it swiftly and without undue complexity.
- Tax filing becomes a less daunting task, with forms pre-populated by the trusted data held within one's digital wallet.
- Casting a vote becomes a secure, digital affirmation of democracy, with the sanctity of every ballot preserved in the digital realm.
- Signing documents, from contracts to applications, is executed with a digital flourish, eliminating the need for pen and paper.

The pivot to such a system, however, hinges on crafting compelling use cases. The wheels of government digitization turn slowly, and the introduction of digital wallets must be both intuitive and necessary to inspire change.

The transformation brought forth by digital wallets in public services is manifold:

- **Citizen Satisfaction:** The eradication of paperwork and the obsolescence of queues transform bureaucratic chores into convenient, digital interactions.
- **Security Enhancement:** With identity fraud siphoning billions from public funds, digital wallets offer a bulwark

of protection, safeguarding the integrity of citizen identities.

- **Civic Engagement:** From digital voting to renewing licenses, wallets can boost citizen participation, weaving the fabric of an engaged society.
- **Fiscal Prudence:** The digitization of public services, as analysed by McKinsey, could unlock savings in the trillions, a financial windfall for governments across the globe.
- **Productivity Surge:** The swift verification of identities digitizes and streamlines processes that once consumed hours of manual effort.

As for the economic framework underpinning digital wallets in public services, the potential is vast:

- **Usage Fees:** Licenses for wallet platforms and credentials could generate a steady revenue stream for service providers.
- **Premium Services:** Enhanced features within digital wallets could cater to citizens seeking added convenience or capabilities.
- **Targeted Advertising:** Wallet apps might host ads, creating a marketplace for civic-minded businesses and services.
- **Data for Policy:** The anonymized aggregate data gleaned from wallet usage can illuminate trends and inform policy decisions.
- **Incentives for Adoption:** Grants and other funding mechanisms can stimulate the uptake of digital wallets, fostering a more digitized public sphere.

The integration of digital wallets into public services represents more than a technological shift—it's a stride towards a future where public services are more accessible, secure, and attuned to the modern citizen's needs. It's a vision of governance that values time, cherishes trust, and embraces the potential of the digital age.

e-Commerce and Retail

In the bustling marketplace of retail, digital wallets are poised to redefine the very essence of shopping, from storefronts to online platforms. These wallets aren't just about payment—they're about crafting an experience that's secure, swift, and satisfying.

Picture a retail world where:

- Online fraud becomes a relic of the past, with transactions safeguarded by the robust security inherent in digital wallets.
- The tap of a phone completes a purchase, transforming in-store payments into a contactless ballet of commerce.
- The hassle of keeping track of physical receipts vanishes, making returns a breeze and convenience the standard.
- Age restrictions on certain purchases are enforced with dignity and ease, thanks to discreet digital verification.
- Loyalty is not just rewarded but integrated, with programs that sync seamlessly with payment processes.

The integration of digital wallets in retail, while brimming with potential, must navigate the intricacies of existing point-of-sale ecosystems. It's a challenge that calls for innovation and adaptation, ensuring that new technology enhances rather than disrupts.

The deployment of identity wallets in the retail sector offers a cascade of benefits:

- **Checkout Streamlining:** The bane of abandoned carts due to cumbersome checkout processes is addressed head-on, with statistics showing a drastic reduction in customer dropout rates.
- **Fraud Mitigation:** With e-commerce bleeding billions to fraud each year, digital wallets offer a shield, securing transactions with their advanced cryptographic frameworks.
- **Customer Experience Enrichment:** A unified customer profile across shopping channels not only simplifies transactions but personalizes the entire retail journey.
- **Innovative Offerings:** From age verification for controlled purchases to new forms of customer engagement, wallets open doors to capabilities once considered futuristic.
- **Basket Size Amplification:** The ease of wallet payments correlates with a significant uptick in average spending, suggesting that convenience could well be the currency of loyalty.

As retailers ponder the monetary models that digital wallets facilitate, the prospects are as varied as they are lucrative:

- **Transaction Fees:** A nominal charge on wallet transactions can underwrite the cost of maintaining secure, seamless services.
- **Commissions on Integrated Services:** Additional offerings, from extended warranties to express shipping, can be neatly woven into the wallet, generating commissions.
- **Verification Tech Licensing:** Biometric technologies that bolster wallet security could be licensed to other entities, opening up new revenue streams.

- **Loyalty Program Subscriptions:** Digital loyalty programs may offer tiered benefits, with subscriptions enhancing the consumer's engagement and rewards.
- **Data-Driven Personalization:** The analytical insights derived from wallet usage could tailor promotions, turning generic ads into personalized invitations.
- **Wallet-Centric Advertising:** The wallet itself could become a platform for advertising, targeting users with relevant offers at the point of payment.

In every thread of the retail industry's fabric, from haute couture to hypermarkets, digital wallets present compelling benefits and revenue opportunities. Yet, their full potential will only be unlocked when retail leaders tackle adoption challenges with strategic acumen, ensuring that digital wallets are not just an option but the preference for consumers worldwide.

Key advantages of identity wallets:

- Lower checkout friction - 94% of customers abandon online retail purchases due to excessive friction
- Reduced fraud - Global e-commerce loses $42 billion to payment fraud annually.
- Better customer experience - Unified view of customer across engagement channels.
- New capabilities - e.g., age verification for controlled purchases.
- Increased basket size - 31% higher for frictionless mobile/wallet payments.
- Accenture estimates that digital identity verification in e-commerce could reduce payment fraud by up to 80%, preventing tens of billions in losses annually.
- The use of digital signatures for e-commerce transactions is associated with 68% higher customer

conversion rates compared to manual signature processes, according to Aberdeen Group.

- 73% of shoppers prefer retailers that use digital verification methods over solely password-based authentication, per data from Signicat.
- Up to 20% of retail customers abandon their shopping carts during checkout due to friction issues when manual authentication is used. Digital verification can substantially reduce this dropout rate.
- Digital ID verification enablement in e-commerce reduces the average time spent to solve fraud-related chargebacks from 14 days to 4 hours, according to data from Mitek.
- Verimi GmbH found that 61% of consumers want to use digital identification methods for online shopping instead of creating new accounts and passwords.
- Aite Group projects that digital identity services will enable over $436 billion in global digital commerce transactions by 2027.
- The use of strong authentication based on digital IDs could eliminate up to 90% of account takeover fraud in e-commerce.

In summary, digital identity solutions in e-commerce can significantly increase customer conversion rates, reduce fraud losses, speed up dispute resolutions, and enhance consumer convenience - ultimately enabling growth of the digital economy. The statistics demonstrate the huge potential impact across the industry.

There are compelling benefits and revenue opportunities across all the major industries. However, realizing the full value depends on overcoming adoption challenges through strategic implementations and compelling use cases.

The Road Ahead

As we stand on the cusp of a digital revolution with European identity wallets at the vanguard, it's crucial to recognize the signposts that will guide us to success. These wallets, a beacon of potential across a myriad of applications, demand not just innovation but a steadfast commitment to a set of pivotal success factors:

- The adoption of a user-centric approach in design is not just beneficial—it's imperative. It ensures that accessibility and usability are not afterthoughts but foundational pillars that uphold the user experience.
- Navigating the maze of regulatory frameworks and compliance mandates is a journey that requires both vigilance and agility. The wallets must stand up to the scrutiny of rigorous standards, safeguarding user interests.
- The inertia of legacy systems, often siloed and entrenched, presents a challenge that calls for a concerted effort to shift towards more agile, integrated infrastructures.
- A strategic eye towards applications where identity wallets can make a significant immediate impact will act as lighthouses, guiding adoption and demonstrating value.
- Collaboration is the lifeblood of this endeavour, where stakeholders from various sectors coalesce around a shared vision, bringing their strengths to the table.
- Lastly, an unwavering commitment to ethics, privacy, and inclusion will ensure that the advancement of technology does not come at the expense of fundamental rights and values.

The road ahead for decentralized identity is indeed steep and demands our collective resilience and wisdom. It's a journey that has the power to redefine security, trust, and convenience within our digital ecosystems. But as we navigate this path, we must do so with our eyes open to the challenges and our hands ready to build bridges over the obstacles we encounter.

Let us embark on this road with the knowledge that while the climb may be arduous, the view from the summit—a landscape of digital harmony and empowerment—will be worth every step.

With diligence and wisdom, decentralized identity can enhance security, trust and convenience across digital ecosystems. But the road ahead remains arduous.

Navigating the Obstacles
Realizing the Promise of Digital Identity Wallets

While the European Identity Wallet promises to revolutionize digital trust and convenience, realizing its ambitious vision requires overcoming complex technological, regulatory, economic and social challenges. This chapter provides an in-depth examination of the key obstacles facing widespread decentralized identity adoption, along with mitigation strategies and solutions to unlock its potential.

The Standardization Labyrinth

A persistent challenge is integrating digital wallets with existing legacy systems across fragmented and siloed contexts. Differences in specifications between wallet providers hampers seamless interoperability.

Proprietary wallet schemes create closed ecosystems and vendor lock-in. Users get confined to specific platforms like Apple Wallet or Alipay, unable to easily port identity data between wallets. This entrenches centralized rather than user-controlled models.

Emerging standards like W3C's Verifiable Credentials remain unstable and unsupported. New protocols and specifications are still maturing across domains. This slows development and adoption.

Bespoke one-off integration efforts are needed for each system a wallet aims to connect with. This causes high costs and delays compared to universal interoperability.

Without solving these standardization issues, the vision of portable user-centric identity wallets hits roadblocks. Creating open standards, common interfaces and vendor-neutral conventions is critical. The EU act aims to mandate interoperability but the technical implementation details remain unclear. Global alignment of standards bodies will also be needed.

Cost and Complexity Barriers

Deploying and operating digital identity wallets requires significant technical expertise and infrastructure costs currently:

- Specialized hardware security modules for cryptographic key management impose high costs for wallet providers and verifiers, especially for small players.
- Redesigning complex legacy IT systems and architectures to interface with wallets requires scarce highly skilled security engineers and developers. The effort can be prohibitive.
- Incorporating biometric systems for user authentication necessitates added backend hardware and software integration work. This includes facial recognition, fingerprint and iris scanning.

Hyperledger Indy estimates 200+ components comprise a blockchain identity wallet, each needing integration and maintenance. This vast complexity limits implementations.

Gradual stepwise pilots using iterative prototyping can help reduce costs and complexity for organizations. Widespread open-source wallet components can also lower barriers to entry and innovation. However, transaction fees or per wallet licensing may be required long-term for ecosystem sustainability as adoption scales.

The Regulatory Compliance Maze

The complex regulatory landscape surrounding digital identity poses technology design and operation challenges:

- eIDAS mandates for wallet standards compatibility, interoperability and security assurance must be met.
- GDPR requires right-to-delete access along with lawful bases for processing and storage built into wallet architectures.
- Diverging country regulations hamper deploying unified identity wallet ecosystems across borders.
- Liability models for identity theft and fraud are legally ambiguous.

Clarifying compliance requirements early for wallet providers is essential, along with standardized security and privacy impact audits. Engaging with policymakers to craft pragmatic regulations can ensure standards match technical realities.

The Immutability Dilemma

User identity claims like credentials are often revocable and time-limited in the physical world. However, blockchains immutably record all transactions indefinitely by design. This creates tensions between the need for evolve-able identity and the permanence of blockchain-based systems.

Legally, this permanence also creates compliance and privacy issues with regulations like GDPR that require erasing data. Technologically, incorporating revocation and expiration mechanisms into immutable ledgers remains challenging.

For specific high-value use cases like contracts or national IDs where irrefutable records are absolutely necessary, blockchain's immutability provides benefits. But more selective contextual use is likely preferable given the downsides. Hybrid on-chain and off-chain architectures may help balance both needs.

The Boundary Spanning Barrier

Successfully launching user-centric identity wallet ecosystems depends profoundly on effective boundary spanning collaboration between public sector agencies, private sector providers, nonprofits, standards bodies and other stakeholders.

This requires committing to create collective boundary resources like:

- Shared semantic data models, schemas and standards for interoperability.
- Aligned incentive models and revenue sharing arrangements.
- Multi-party governance mechanisms enabling ecosystem coordination and evolution.
- Legal and regulatory frameworks facilitating innovation.

Proactively developing these boundary spanning resources and partnerships can catalyse adoption by unblocking cooperation barriers across sectors. This reduces innovation risks and fosters trust.

But absence of incentives alignment, governance and resources creates a catch-22 impeding progress.

The Social Risks Landmine

While promising, digital identity frameworks also carry risks of exacerbating social inequalities and loss of privacy freedoms if not thoughtfully implemented:

- Digital exclusion arises if solutions mandate smartphones or biometrics that many citizens lack reliable access to.
- Surveillance risks emerge from vast aggregation of personal identity data across contexts.

- Validity of user consent becomes questionable given adoption pressures from governments and services providers. Users may have little choice but to accept.
- Opaqueness around how personal data gets used once inside wallets leads to transparency concerns.
- Potential arises for increasing state or corporate control over citizens through identity tools.

A nuanced, ethical approach considering social impacts will be imperative for decentralized identity to avoid these dangerous pitfalls. The technology itself does not predetermine outcomes - it depends on how it gets applied in practice. But these risks spotlight the need for caution and vigilance.

Overcoming Hurdles Through Holistic Innovation

While decentralized digital identity promises significant upside, realizing its constructive potential requires proactively addressing persistent technological, regulatory, economic, legal and social challenges. With diligence, collaboration and wisdom, policymakers and innovators can chart a course that maximizes widespread trust and empowerment from identity wallets while minimizing harm. But simple technical fixes are insufficient - holistic socio-technical innovation spanning sectors, disciplines and worldviews is imperative. The destination is worth the obstacles along the way.

Managing the Risks and Accountability

In a world that's increasingly digital, the concept of identity has undergone significant transformation. The European Identity Wallet aims to be a cornerstone in this new landscape, providing a unified, secure means of managing digital identity across the continent. While the promise is immense—simplifying bureaucratic processes, enhancing cybersecurity, and offering a seamless user experience—the challenges and risks are equally formidable.

This chapter delves into the labyrinth of risks that accompany the implementation of the European Identity Wallet, both for organizations that adopt it and for the individuals who will ultimately use it. Our intention is not merely to outline these risks but to serve as a practical guide. This chapter is designed to help organizations and individuals critically think about how to address these issues, counteract them, and formulate policies to protect themselves.

With rapidly evolving technological paradigms, such as blockchain, at the heart of these new identity systems, the risks are multifaceted. They range from legal and regulatory dilemmas like GDPR compliance, to ethical quandaries such as data misuse and the potential for increasing social inequality. We will also examine concerns around security vulnerabilities, from the possibility of identity theft to the challenges of key management.

By dissecting these issues, this chapter aims to offer a comprehensive understanding of what's at stake. For organizations, understanding these risks is crucial for compliance, reputation management, and ultimately, the trust of their users. For individuals, it is a matter of personal security, privacy, and the integrity of one's digital self in an interconnected world.

We'll propose potential mitigations and policy recommendations. Whether you're a policy-maker, a technologist, or an end-user, navigating this terrain with a well-informed compass is not just advisable; it's imperative. Stay with us as we unravel the complex tapestry of risks, laying bare the challenges while offering actionable insights to safeguard your digital identity in this new frontier

Consolidated Risk Analysis of the European Identity Wallet

For the User:

The Landscape: As users, we're entering a new era where our personal data is the key to seamless services. However, it's natural to feel cautious — the centralization of our data could attract unwanted attention from cybercriminals, putting our privacy at risk.

User Perspective:

Risk Type	Description	Mitigation Strategies
Privacy	Centralization of data could make the wallet a target for cyber-attacks, leading to identity theft.	Use advanced encryption, limit data sharing, implement strict access controls.
Security	A compromised system could result in leaked personal information.	Adhere to security best practices, conduct regular audits, and engage in thorough penetration testing.
Reliability	System downtimes could lock users out, limiting access to services.	Develop alternative access methods and decentralized identifiers for redundancy.
Misuse	Credentials might be used without consent, leading to unauthorized access.	Deploy multi-factor authentication, maintain audit logs, and utilize anomaly detection.

Complia nce	Users may have limited control over how their data is shared.	Enhance transparency, provide fine-grained consent options, and ensure privacy guarantees.

Navigating the Terrain: To safeguard our digital selves, encryption is our shield, minimizing data sharing is our strategy, and strict access controls are our guards. Should the system face a threat, regular security checks and a robust fallback plan ensure we're never left stranded. Our digital credentials are ours alone, protected by layers of authentication and vigilant monitoring. And when it comes to compliance, transparency isn't just a buzzword; it's our right, guaranteed by fine-grained consent controls.

For the Government:

The Challenge: As stewards of the national digital landscape, the government faces the formidable task of protecting a centralized system against cyber threats. Implementing such a cross-border wallet system is like orchestrating a symphony — it requires precision, patience, and a keen ear for harmony.

Government Perspective:

Risk Type	Description	Mitigation Strategies
Cyber-security	A centralized system presents a high-value target for hackers, necessitating robust security measures.	Develop a comprehensive security strategy with layered defences.
Operation al	Implementing a cross-border system within the EU presents complex challenges.	Employ a phased pilot approach, test for scalability, and ensure multi-party cooperation and dependencies.
Adoption	Potential resistance from citizens may hinder the	Conduct citizen education initiatives, highlight

	adoption of the wallet.	benefits, and offer incentives to encourage adoption.
Fraud	There is a risk of exploitation by malicious parties.	Implement identity proofing, risk-based authentication, and continuous fraud monitoring systems.
Standardization	Aligning standards for identity attributes and architecture across the EU is challenging.	Engage all stakeholders in the standardization process to achieve consensus.

Strategic Measures: A comprehensive security strategy fortified with layered defences serves as our bulwark. A phased rollout approach, akin to test flights before the maiden voyage, ensures reliability and scalability. To foster adoption, we become educators and advocates, championing the wallet's benefits with clear incentives. Fraud monitoring systems act as our sentinels, ever-watchful against misuse.

For the Service Provider:

The Opportunity: For service providers, the wallet is a bridge to efficiency and enhanced customer service. But this bridge needs careful construction — integration costs and operational dependencies must be meticulously managed.

Service Provider Perspective:

Risk Type	Description	Mitigation Strategies
Integration Cost	Significant development is needed to integrate systems with the wallet, incurring high costs.	Provide technical integration support, adopt open standards, and offer reference architectures.
Reliability	Service providers rely on the wallet's availability	Establish Service Level Agreements (SLAs),

	and resilience for their services.	ensure system redundancy, and decouple integrations.
Compliance	Service providers must align with the standards and processes associated with wallet usage.	Clearly define usage policies, establish validation mechanisms, and adhere to compliance standards.
Loss of Control	Managing user data externally means providers have less control and visibility.	Create dashboards for visibility and allow for advanced integration options.
Lock-in Risk	Dependency on the wallet system could make it difficult to switch or rollback its use.	Ensure standard integrations and maintain the ability to choose alternate providers.

Building Blocks for Success: Support and open standards ease the integration process, while service level agreements and redundancy plans provide a safety net. Clear policies and validation mechanisms ensure compliance, and advanced integration options give providers the control they desire. To avoid lock-in, we champion flexibility, ensuring that there's always a choice in how we connect and operate.

Consolidating the Perspectives:

When we weave together the threads from all viewpoints, a tapestry of shared concerns emerges, featuring privacy, security, and the smooth operation of the wallet at its core. For users, it's about trust and ease of use. For governments, it's about robust security and seamless service delivery. For service providers, it's about integrating seamlessly and maintaining control.

The Road Ahead:

The journey ahead with the European Identity Wallet is indeed promising. With strong encryption, meticulous access controls, and a commitment to open standards, we can navigate the risks. A tailored approach — with an eye on security, a focus on user-centric design, and a drive for operational excellence — will lead to a successful implementation.

Example Scenario: Identity Verification Using European Identity Wallet vs. mob.id

Scenario with European Identity Wallet:

In this scenario, a citizen is walking down the street when a police officer stops them for an identity check. The officer takes out his smartphone, displaying a QR code, and requests the civilian to identify themselves by scanning the code. The citizen, complying with the request, scans the QR code using their smartphone, which triggers their European Identity Wallet to share the required identity information with the officer.

Challenges:

- **Verification of Officer's Identity:** The citizen has limited means to verify if the person requesting the information is indeed a legitimate police officer.
- **Privilege Verification:** There's no immediate way for the citizen to know if the officer has the necessary privileges to request and receive such information.
- **Consent Verification:** While the citizen consents by scanning the QR code, the process lacks an additional verification layer to reinforce trust and security.

Scenario with mob.id:

In contrast, let's consider the same situation but with the citizen using mob.id for identity verification.

- **Initial Interaction:** A police officer stops the citizen and requests identification. The officer presents a QR code to be scanned by the citizen.
- **Out-of-Band Verification:** As soon as the citizen scans the QR code with their mob.id app, an out-of-band check is initiated. This check verifies the officer's identity and their credentials to request identity information.
- **Mutual Authentication:** To enhance trust, the citizens and the officer's passport photos are displayed on each other's smartphones. They visually confirm if the person they are interacting with matches the photo displayed. This step ensures that both parties are indeed who they claim to be, without exchanging further information.
- **Informed Consent:** Once the citizen is satisfied with the verification, they can confidently give consent for the information exchange. This consent is informed and based on a clear understanding of who is receiving their data and for what purpose.
- **Data Exchange:** Upon receiving consent, the necessary identity information is securely transmitted from the citizens mob.id to the officer's device.

The mob.id scenario offers a more robust and secure approach to identity verification in public settings. It addresses the key challenges of verifying the identity and privileges of the officer, ensuring that the citizens consent is informed and genuine. This method not only enhances privacy and trust but also empowers the citizen in the exchange, making it a preferred approach for secure and transparent identity verification in real-life situations.

As managers, our mission is clear. We must steer this ship with a steady hand, ensuring that each measure, from encryption to education, is not just implemented but ingrained in our approach. Let's embark on this journey with confidence, knowing that together, we can realize the vision of a digital identity system that's as secure as it is empowering.

Trust Model Complexity

The European Identity Wallet's trust model is layered with complexities, encompassing trust anchors, biometry, and biographical attributes. These elements have varying states of presence and reliability, leading to 17 different outcome scenarios. Only one scenario represents a fully trustworthy situation. This analysis explores the risks involved in each component from both the attestation and derived identity perspectives.

Trust Anchor Risks:

Trust Anchor Not Present or Unreliable:

- **Attestation Risk:** If the trust anchor is absent or not reliable, the entire foundation of the identity is questionable.
- **Derived Identity Risk:** An unreliable trust anchor undermines the legitimacy of the derived identity.

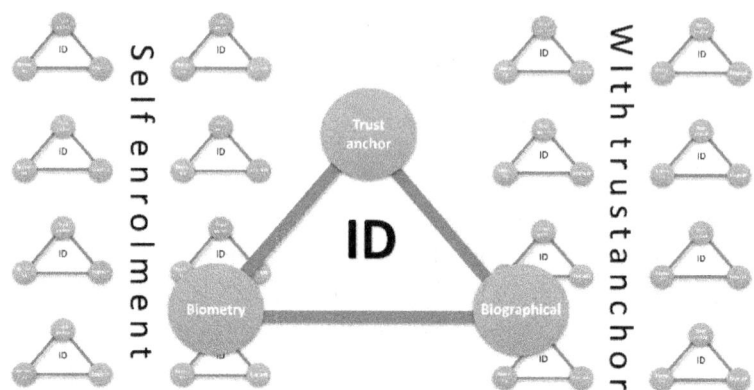

17 identities

- **Countermeasures:** Implement fail-safes for detecting the absence or compromise of trust anchors and mechanisms to re-establish trust.

Trust Anchor Present and Reliable:

- **Attestation Risk:** Even with a reliable trust anchor, risks persist in data transmission and storage.
- **Derived Identity Risk:** Overreliance on trust anchors might lead to neglecting other security measures.
- **Countermeasures:** Maintain holistic security measures beyond trust anchors and ensure end-to-end encryption in data handling.

Biometric Verification Risks:

Biometry Absent or Not Properly Verified:

- **Attestation Risk:** Incorrect biometric data leads to false identity verification.
- **Derived Identity Risk:** Lacks a personal, non-repudiable link to the individual.

- **Countermeasures:** Employ secondary verification methods and regular updates to biometric systems.

Biometry Present and Verified:

- **Attestation Risk:** Possibility of biometric spoofing or data breaches.
- **Derived Identity Risk:** Overdependence on biometrics might ignore other security aspects.
- **Countermeasures:** Use multi-modal biometrics and continuous monitoring for anomalies.

Biographical Data Risks:

Biographical Data Inaccurate or Not Verified:

- **Attestation Risk:** False or outdated information undermines the identity's accuracy.
- **Derived Identity Risk:** Misrepresentation of the individual's identity.
- **Countermeasures:** Regular data validation checks and user ability to update their information.

Biographical Data Accurate and Verified:

- **Attestation Risk:** Risks of data leakage or misuse by third parties.
- **Derived Identity Risk:** Accurate data can still be vulnerable to unauthorized access.
- **Countermeasures:** Strict data access controls and regular privacy audits.

Navigating the Trust Matrix

Understanding the different scenarios of trust anchor, biometry, and biographical data in the European Identity Wallet is crucial for identifying potential risks. Each component's state – whether present, absent, reliable, or unreliable – creates a unique set of challenges. The only fully trustworthy scenario is where all components are present and reliable, both in the attestation and the derived identity.

For managers and stakeholders, the key is to not only focus on achieving this ideal scenario but also to have robust countermeasures for less-than-ideal situations. Regular system audits, multi-modal security strategies, and ensuring user empowerment in managing their data are crucial. By navigating this trust matrix thoughtfully, the European Identity Wallet can be a secure, reliable, and user-centric solution in the digital identity landscape.

The Convenience Quandary

The European Identity Wallet is undoubtedly a remarkable innovation. It streamlines various processes, from travel to healthcare and beyond, into one unified, digital system. It promises more seamless interactions with governmental and private sectors alike. But what happens when something designed to make life easier also makes illicit activities easier for fraudsters?

The Small Charge Strategy

Imagine this scenario: you come across an appealing service, offering a lifetime subscription to an exclusive online platform. They support the European Identity Wallet, making the sign-up process a breeze. What you don't know, however, is that the service is a sham. Now a malicious entity has all the information they need to impersonate you.

You might think that a large, noticeable fraud attempt will follow, but sophisticated criminals go for the long con. They might start setting up small, recurring payments from your account. The amount is negligible—just enough to escape your notice but substantial over time.

Legal Framework: Is It Enough?

In theory, the law is on the side of identity theft victims. But the practicalities of recovering from identity fraud are both stressful and time-consuming. More importantly, the perpetrators are notoriously difficult to catch. The legal system is generally not fast enough to keep up with the speed at which these criminals operate.

The Fine Print Problem

A standard defence for organizations is claiming that the user agreed to share their information, often pointing to 'terms and conditions' that nobody bothers to read. If the large majority of people don't read the fine print, is it ethical—or even legal—to hold them accountable for what's hidden in there?

A Call for More Secure Measures

If we recognize that the European Identity Wallet has the potential to make identity theft easier, shouldn't we then consider more robust security measures? Should we be questioning a system that, by virtue of making life more convenient, also makes it easier for people to fall victim to identity fraud?

Thoughts

While the European Identity Wallet aims to be a game-changer in how we manage our identities, it also raises significant questions about security and ethics. As we move towards increasingly digital lives, we must be diligent in evaluating both the promises and the risks that come with these advancements.

By understanding these pitfalls, we can hope to adapt the system to better protect its users, making sure that convenience does not compromise security.

Below is a hypothetical example of how a company might ambiguously request sensitive information within the context of the European Identity Wallet. It's important to note that practices like this could be misleading or even illegal depending on jurisdiction, and this example is for illustrative purposes only.

Registration Form: EuroExclusive VIP Experience

☐ Welcome to EuroExclusive! Enjoy premier access to European luxury, travel, and cultural experiences. We are proud to support the new European Identity Wallet. It's faster, safer, and more convenient.

Step 1: Basic Information

➢ First Name: _____

➢ Last Name: _____

➢ Email: _____

Step 2: Confirm Your European Identity Wallet Credentials

> *To ensure that we are offering these*
> *exclusive services to genuine European*
> *citizens and residents, please consent to*
> *sharing your European Identity Wallet data*
> *with us.*

➢ Date of Birth: _____

➢ Address: _____

➢ National Identification Number: _____

> *Your trust is our top priority. All your data*
> *is securely encrypted and stored in*
> *compliance with European regulations.*

Step 3: Consent and Proceed

By ticking the box below, you agree to our Privacy Policy and Terms of Service. This will allow EuroExclusive to utilize your European Identity Wallet data for internal purposes, service customization, and as may be required by applicable laws and regulations.

[ ] I consent to sharing my European Identity Wallet data and agree to EuroExclusive's Privacy Policy and Terms of Service.

The form includes terms like "for internal purposes" and "as may be required by applicable laws and regulations" but does not provide specific details on how the sensitive information, like your National Identification Number, might be used. This kind of language could potentially mislead people into sharing information without fully understanding the implications.

Always make sure to read and understand the fine print when you are consenting to share sensitive information.

I am not a legal expert, but generally speaking, the ambiguous language in the hypothetical example, such as "for internal purposes" and "as may be required by applicable laws and regulations," could create a loophole. However, in most countries, opening a bank account or taking out a loan in someone else's name without explicit consent would be considered identity theft or fraud.

Legitimate companies that intend to use your identity information to open bank accounts, apply for loans, or engage in any other kind of financial transaction on your behalf would need to get your explicit consent for those specific actions. These consents are often detailed and separate from a general term of service or privacy policy. If the company used the data for such purposes without explicit consent for those activities, they could potentially be liable for identity fraud or other illegal activities.

Always be careful when providing sensitive personal information and be sure to read and understand any associated terms and conditions or privacy policies. When in doubt, consult with legal advisors or other professionals.

So, the next questions are: Is it possible for an illegitimate company to exploit the European Identity Wallet to establish recurring low-value transactions, designed to evade detection?

The Small Charge Strategy

Imagine this scenario: you come across an appealing service, offering a lifetime subscription to an exclusive online platform. They support the European Identity Wallet, making the sign-up process a breeze. What you don't know, however, is that the service is a sham. Now a malicious entity has all the information they need to impersonate you.

You might think that a large, noticeable fraud attempt will follow, but sophisticated criminals go for the long con. They might start setting up small, recurring payments from your account. The amount is negligible—just enough to escape your notice but substantial over time.

Legal Framework: Is It Enough?

In theory, the law is on the side of identity theft victims. But the practicalities of recovering from identity fraud are both stressful and time-consuming. More importantly, the perpetrators are notoriously difficult to catch. The legal system is generally not fast enough to keep up with the speed at which these criminals operate.

The Fine Print Problem

A standard defence for organizations is claiming that the user agreed to share their information, often pointing to 'terms and conditions' that nobody bothers to read. If the large majority of people don't read the fine print, is it ethical—or even legal—to hold them accountable for what's hidden in there?

A Call for More Secure Measures

If we recognize that the European Identity Wallet has the potential to make identity theft easier, shouldn't we then consider more robust security measures? Should we be questioning a system that, by virtue of making life more convenient, also makes it easier for people to fall victim to identity fraud?

While the European Identity Wallet aims to be a game-changer in how we manage our identities, it also raises significant questions about security and ethics. As we move towards increasingly digital lives, we must be diligent in evaluating both the promises and the risks that come with these advancements.

By understanding these pitfalls, we can hope to adapt the system to better protect its users, making sure that convenience does not compromise security.

The Double-Edged Sword of the European Identity Wallet and Blockchain Technology

The Convenience Quandary

The European Identity Wallet promises seamless interactions with a variety of services, both governmental and private. But there's a downside—such ease can also simplify the job of fraudsters. And what if we add blockchain into the mix? This chapter aims to unpack the potential risks involved, considering not just the wallet itself but also the underlying technology that could power it.

Blockchain: A Mixed Blessing

Using blockchain technology for European identity management presents both opportunities and risks. Below are some of the risks associated with such an application:

Regulatory Compliance

> **GDPR:** Blockchain's immutable nature could potentially conflict with GDPR's "right to be forgotten," which mandates that personal data should be erasable.

> **Legal Recognition:** Some countries may not recognize blockchain-based identity systems as valid forms of identification.

Security Concerns

> **51% Attacks:** Although unlikely in well-distributed networks, a single entity gaining control of over 50% of the network could manipulate the data.

> **Smart Contract Vulnerabilities:** If identity management involves smart contracts, those could have vulnerabilities that can be exploited.

➤ **Key Management:** Losing access to private keys can mean losing access to one's identity. Conversely, if someone gains unauthorized access to your private key, they essentially "become" you.

Technological Barriers

➤ **Interoperability:** Blockchain solutions often suffer from compatibility issues with other systems.

➤ **Complexity and Usability:** The general public might find blockchain-based systems more complex and harder to use than traditional systems.

Social and Ethical Concerns

➤ **Inequality:** People without access to technology could be excluded from such a system, exacerbating social inequalities.

➤ **Surveillance Risks:** While blockchain can provide anonymity, it can also be designed to be excessively intrusive.

Economic Barriers

➤ **Cost:** Building and maintaining a blockchain can be expensive.

➤ **Adoption:** Getting widespread adoption for a new form of identity verification can be slow and costly.

The Fine Print Problem

A common defence for organizations is that the user agreed to share their information, usually via unread 'terms and conditions.' This raises ethical and possibly even legal questions, particularly when we consider that most people don't read these documents.

A Call for Robust Measures

As we embrace new technologies like the European Identity Wallet and potentially blockchain, we should be extra cautious. While they offer many benefits, they also come with their own set of complications and vulnerabilities.

In the quest for convenience and efficiency, we mustn't overlook the imperative of security and ethics. As our lives become increasingly digital, the trade-offs become more significant and potentially more damaging. Understanding these complexities can guide us toward creating systems that offer the best of both worlds without compromising our values or safety. Given the regulatory environment in Europe and the critical nature of identity management, any implementation needs to be carefully planned and executed.

By examining these challenges, industry professionals, including those working on solutions like mob.id, can better navigate the complexities of modern identity management. This balanced approach will ensure that innovation doesn't come at the cost of security or social equity.

The Question of Accountability in Blockchain-Based Identity Management

The Accountability Conundrum

Accountability is a critical concern when considering the use of blockchain for identity management systems. The decentralized nature of blockchain technology presents both advantages and challenges in this regard.

Challenges

Immutable Records: Once a transaction is added to a blockchain, it can't be changed. If someone steals or misuses another person's identity, that record is permanently on the blockchain. This could have legal implications and could be especially problematic if the system is designed to automatically execute actions based on identity verification.

Private Key Management: If an individual's private key is stolen, it can be difficult to prove theft or misuse since transactions will appear legitimate. This could lead to a lack of accountability because the system inherently trusts the holder of the private key.

Jurisdictional Issues: In a global, decentralized network, it could be challenging to enforce legal actions or determine jurisdiction for crimes committed across borders.

Possible Solutions

Multi-Factor Authentication: Implementing additional layers of security can help mitigate the risks of identity theft.

Smart Contracts for Monitoring: Smart contracts could be programmed to flag or halt suspicious activities, making it easier to intervene when identity misuse appears to occur.

Off-Chain Governance: Procedures for identity verification and dispute resolution could be managed off-chain, integrating with the blockchain only once an issue has been resolved. However, this requires a trusted centralized entity, somewhat negating the point of decentralization.

Legal Framework: A clearly defined legal framework that applies to blockchain identity verification could outline responsibilities and penalties, providing a means for legal redress in case of identity theft or misuse.

User Education: Educating users about best practices for private key management and overall security can go a long way in preventing misuse.

Auditing and Forensics: While the blockchain is immutable, it is also transparent and can be audited. With sufficient off-chain information, it might be possible to prove misuse forensically, even if it can't be changed on-chain.

Anchoring Identity: Binding the blockchain identity to a legally recognized form of ID in a secure way can provide a backstop in cases where blockchain-based identity is stolen or misused.

Navigating the Accountability Landscape

Accountability mechanisms would need to be built into the architecture of any blockchain-based identity system, and legal systems may need to adapt to be able to effectively deal with challenges presented by this new technology. This complexity adds another layer to the already intricate puzzle of modern identity management. Given the European regulatory landscape and the critical nature of identity, companies like mob.id that are operating in this space would need to consider these challenges and solutions deeply in the design and deployment of identity management solutions.

A Balanced Equation

In essence, the use of blockchain in the European Identity Wallet is a complex equation with multiple variables, ranging from technological considerations to ethical concerns. Striking the right balance is a formidable task that requires active collaboration among technologists, policymakers, and legal experts. It's a journey filled with both promise and pitfalls, and navigating it will define the future of digital identity in Europe and potentially the rest of the world.

Realizing decentralized identity's potential requires navigating complex risks and accountability gaps. This chapter examines legal, technical and ethical tensions, along with potential mitigation strategies for both managers and legal teams.

The Permanence Paradox

A benefit of blockchain-based identity systems is providing permanent tamper-proof transaction records. However, conflicts arise between this immutable permanence and real-world identity dynamics:

- GDPR "right to be forgotten" is obstructed by blockchains' indelible records. This exposes organizations to compliance risks and steep fines up to 4% of global revenue.
- Investigations requiring flexible evidence preservation mechanisms are hindered.
- Identity attributes and credentials evolve, requiring adaptability versus permanent ledgers.

Proposed technical solutions balance immutability and identity fluidity via metadata pointers, off-chain storage, and permissioned editing. But reconciling this paradox may require rethinking legal frameworks and organizational policies. Managers must collaborate with legal teams to navigate tensions.

The Private Key Pitfall

With self-sovereign identity models, private keys enabling access and control become a central point of vulnerability. If compromised, identity systems are undermined despite blockchain protections:

- Ownership ambiguity makes legal responsibility unclear - who owns a private key? The user, wallet provider or collective stakeholders? This grey area requires policy clarification.
- Proving criminal misuse is challenging since stolen keys appear technically legitimate from a system perspective. Burden of proof complications have legal implications.
- Without centralized oversight, liability assigning for key misuse grows uncertain. An example is recovering assets after lost private keys.

While hardware wallets and multi-factor authentication improve security, fundamentally reassessing liability models is also needed. Exploring identity insurance frameworks that allocate risks appropriately through clear policies can help provide accountability.

The Jurisdictional Maze

Decentralized architectures create jurisdictional uncertainties given global identities and transactions:

- Determining applicable laws grows complex with cross-border identity ecosystems. This can impede legal recourse.
- Differing user and provider locations compound jurisdictional ambiguities.
- Transactions involving multiple parties across countries add complexity.
- Anonymity and decentralization obstruct enforcement. Regulators may be unable to intervene.

While common identity standards aid interoperability, substantial policy gaps remain regarding disputes and redress across borders. Reconciling conflicting regulations is extremely difficult but necessary to ensure accountability.

The Redress Riddle

Seeking legal recourse for identity misuse on blockchains faces systemic roadblocks:

- Limited accessible logs and ambiguous evidence trails. This opacity impedes investigations.
- Unclear liability with decentralized architectures. Victims may have no legal recourse.
- Few enforcement mechanisms within blockchain ecosystems currently. Judgments may be unenforceable.
- Often prohibitive legal costs for individuals. Justice remains inaccessible.

Managers must collaborate with legal teams and policymakers to enact reforms addressing these accountability gaps through regulation, governance and education.

With diligence and wisdom, organizations can develop nuanced governance and technical mitigation strategies that thoughtfully balance decentralization's advantages while ensuring accountability. But acknowledging uncharted risks is essential, rather than assuming technology alone fosters fair outcomes.

Cultivating Inclusivity

In an era where digitalization is rapidly reshaping societal interactions, the imperative for equitable access to digital resources has never been more critical. This Chapter delves into the heart of inclusivity within the European digital identity framework, unravelling the complexities and championing the cause for a universally accessible and fair digital ecosystem.

As the European Union strides towards the integration of digital identity across its member states, the vision for a seamless, secure, and efficient online experience faces the stark reality of the digital divide. This chapter confronts this divide head-on, exploring the multifaceted challenges that certain marginalized groups face in accessing and utilizing digital identity platforms. It also lays bare the societal and systemic structures that perpetuate this divide.

From individuals experiencing homelessness to the variegated tapestry of minorities and immigrants, and not forgetting those with limited formal education, the chapter casts a light on those who stand at the peripheries of the digital revolution. Drawing upon a wealth of scholarly research, case studies, and expert insights, we explore the contours of these challenges within the European context, providing managers with a profound understanding of the digital landscape they navigate.

This chapter is not merely a narrative of challenges; it is a blueprint for action. It outlines strategic, actionable solutions that managers can implement to foster inclusivity. Through a close examination of initiatives like WiFi4EU, language-specific programs in Barcelona, and the EU's Digital Education Action Plan, we offer a template for building a more inclusive digital Europe. By highlighting best practices and sharing success stories, we aim to empower leaders to become architects of change, equipped to dismantle barriers and build bridges in the digital domain.

In pursuit of a digital identity ecosystem that truly reflects the diverse fabric of European society, this chapter is both a call to action and a guiding light. It invites managers to embark on a journey of transformation, one that champions inclusivity, upholds dignity, and paves the way for a more connected and inclusive Europe.

Ensuring Equitable Technology Access in Europe

In the quest for a cohesive European digital identity, ensuring equitable technology access is a cornerstone. This section scrutinizes the challenges and unveils solutions to bridge the digital divide that prevents marginalized groups from fully participating in the digital landscape.

Individuals Experiencing Homelessness

Across Europe, homelessness presents a significant obstacle to digital inclusivity. The European Federation of National Organisations Working with the Homeless (FEANTSA) underscores the importance of technology in aiding social inclusion for these individuals. In Finland, the initiative by VAILLA VAKINAISTA ASUNTOA RY (Vva), which offers digital literacy programs, provides a replicable model. Vva was founded in 1986 by homeless people themselves, when there were 20 000 homeless persons in Finland. Now the number is 3686. Today Vva has about 40 employees working in various areas of service. About 30 percent of our employees have first-hand experience of homelessness.

Managers can draw inspiration from such programs and introduce mobile access points and flexible verification processes that do not rely solely on fixed addresses.

"Connectivity can be a lifeline for those without a home, offering a bridge to essential services and social inclusion." – Expert from FEANTSA.

Minorities and Immigrants The digital gap for minorities and immigrants in Europe is significant. Language barriers, cultural disconnects, and economic disparities often stand in the way of these communities and their access to digital resources. The "Digital Empowerment" initiative in Barcelona provides a model for addressing this, offering tailored training that respects cultural nuances. Managers should consider such bespoke solutions, ensuring that digital identity systems are both accessible and relevant to these diverse groups.

"Diversity in digital access is more than a technical issue; it's a reflection of our commitment to an inclusive society." –
Frans Bolk Founder mob.id.

Persons with Limited Formal Education Educational attainment is a predictor of digital literacy. The European Commission's Digital Education Action Plan emphasizes the need for digital competencies for all. Managers can respond by providing training that meets individuals at their level of understanding, perhaps through gamified learning platforms that make technology approachable and engaging.

Managerial Solutions for Digital Inclusivity Managers have a toolkit of strategies to enhance digital inclusivity:

- Conduct Equal Access Audits: Regular audits based on the European standard EN 301 549 can identify and resolve inclusivity barriers. This proactive measure ensures that digital identity systems are accessible to all, regardless of their socio-economic status.

- Establish Community Tech Hubs: By setting up tech hubs, organizations can provide a physical space for marginalized individuals to learn about and access digital identities. These hubs can serve as a model for inclusive design and support.
- Create Multilingual Platforms: Reflecting Europe's linguistic diversity, digital platforms must operate in multiple languages. Managers can look to the EU's eJustice portal as a benchmark for multilingual digital service provision.
- Forge Non-Profit Partnerships: Collaborations with organizations like "All Digital" harness community trust and resources, amplifying the reach and impact of digital identity services.

Overcoming Potential Roadblocks While the path to digital inclusivity is clear, it's not without its obstacles. Managers must navigate funding limitations, bureaucratic inertia, and varying levels of digital literacy. To overcome these, securing EU funding, fostering innovation, and ensuring GDPR compliance are crucial. By addressing these challenges, managers can lead the charge towards a digital identity framework that embodies the inclusive spirit of Europe.

Upholding Consent and Autonomy in Digital Identity Systems

Securing individual consent is fundamental in deploying digital identity systems, particularly in Europe, where privacy and personal autonomy are highly valued. This section examines the societal pressures that can undermine consent and offers strategies to uphold individual choice within the European digital identity framework.

Private Sector Influence and User Consent

In Europe, businesses often pioneer digital innovation, but their policies may unduly influence user choices. For instance, certain services might require individuals to subscribe to their digital ID platforms, impeding the autonomy of choice. The European Union's General Data Protection Regulation (GDPR) provides a regulatory backdrop that managers can use as a benchmark to ensure private sector policies do not compromise voluntary consent.

"While businesses drive digital utility, it is imperative that user consent remains a voluntary pillar, not one eroded by corporate mandates."

Digital-Only Services and the Right to Choose

The shift towards digital-only services is accelerating in Europe, potentially marginalizing those who either cannot or choose not to engage digitally. The European Commission's Digital Inclusion and Engagement policy underscores the necessity of maintaining alternative access to services. Managers should ensure that digital identity systems include analogue options to cater to all users.

"Digital inclusivity means providing options, not restrictions. Users should have the freedom to opt for non-digital channels if they prefer."

Strategies for Preserving Consent

To protect user autonomy in the European digital landscape, managers can implement the following strategies:

- **Legislate User Rights:** Advocate for policies that protect users' rights to access services with or without digital identities, drawing from GDPR principles.
- **Opt-Out Mechanisms:** Develop simple and accessible processes that allow users to opt-out or revoke their digital identities, ensuring that consent is continuous and can be withdrawn at any time.
- **Alternate Identity Providers:** Support the use of credentials from multiple identity providers to avoid monopolies and ensure users have a choice in determining the most suitable option for their needs.

"Consent is not a one-time transaction but an ongoing choice. Upholding it requires constant vigilance and adaptability in our policies and systems."

Navigating the Challenges

Implementing these strategies can meet resistance, whether from entrenched business interests or from technological inertia. Managers must balance the push for digital advancement with the preservation of individual rights. Adopting a user-centric approach, engaging with stakeholders, and promoting transparency are key to navigating these challenges successfully.

By emphasizing consent and autonomy, managers will not only align with European values but will also foster trust and acceptance of digital identity systems, ensuring they are truly for the benefit of all Europeans.

Navigating Surveillance Risks in Digital Identity with PKI and Blockchain Considerations

In Europe's digital identity landscape, maintaining privacy while ensuring security is a complex challenge. Public Key Infrastructure (PKI) and blockchain are two technologies at the forefront of this challenge, each with its strengths and potential vulnerabilities. This section contrasts PKI with blockchain technology, evaluates their respective risks, and provides guidance for managers on implementing a robust digital identity system that aligns with European privacy standards.

PKI as a Traditional Stronghold for Digital Identity

PKI is a well-established technology for securing electronic transactions and communications through the use of digital certificates and cryptographic key pairs. It is the backbone of many current digital identity systems, including the issuance of electronic passports and other government ID documents. The strength of PKI lies in its proven track record and the ability to isolate breaches to individual certificates, limiting the scope of any given security incident.

> *"PKI has been the cornerstone of digital*
> *security for decades, providing a tried-and-*
> *tested framework for identity verification*
> *and encryption."*

Case Study: The implementation of PKI in electronic passports (ePassports) in the EU provides each document with a unique digital signature, preventing counterfeiting and unauthorized reading of the RFID chip contained within.

Blockchain Technology: Advantages and Risks

Blockchain technology, often heralded for its decentralization and security, brings a new dimension to digital identity systems. It disperses data across a network, making it more resilient against centralized attacks. However, blockchain is not without risks. If control over a blockchain network is compromised, which can happen through a 51% attack or vulnerabilities in smart contracts, the integrity of the entire system can be at stake.

"While blockchain offers exciting opportunities for decentralization, its security is contingent on the robustness of its network and the smart contracts that govern it."

Comparing PKI and Blockchain Risks

With PKI, the risks are often more localized. If a hacker compromises a single digital certificate, only the information associated with that certificate is at risk. In contrast, blockchain's risks are systemic. A successful attack on the system could potentially compromise the data integrity of all users. However, the likelihood and feasibility of such a widespread blockchain attack remain debated among experts.

Case Study: The Estonian government utilizes both PKI and blockchain for its e-Residency program. The PKI secures individual identities, while blockchain ensures the integrity of public records.

Strategic Implementation for Managers

Managers considering these technologies must weigh the pros and cons in the context of their specific needs and regulatory constraints.

Risk Assessment: Conduct thorough risk assessments for both PKI and blockchain technologies, considering the potential impact of breaches on a systemic versus individual level.

Compliance with GDPR: Ensure that any implemented technology complies with GDPR requirements, particularly the principles of data minimization and the right to erasure, which can be more challenging with blockchain.

Balancing Technology with Policy: Develop policies that balance the use of technology with traditional security measures, such as physical verification processes that complement digital systems.

> *"To effectively protect European citizens'*
> *privacy, we must create a digital identity*
> *system that leverages the strengths of PKI*
> *and blockchain, while also being fully aware*
> *of and prepared for their respective risks.".*

Conclusion: Assessing Surveillance Risks in Digital Identity Systems with PKI and Blockchain

As European entities navigate the intricate waters of digital identity management, they must make critical decisions on the technology that underpins these systems. Both Public Key Infrastructure (PKI) and blockchain technologies offer unique advantages and bear distinct surveillance risks. However, the decision between these technologies is not merely a technical one; it is fundamentally about aligning with European values of privacy, security, and individual rights.

PKI, with its centralized nature, has been a stalwart in digital security for many years. Its structured approach to digital certificates and keys is a testament to its reliability and trustworthiness in verifying identities securely. The risks associated with PKI are more contained; when a breach occurs, it usually impacts a single user. This containment aligns with the European focus on individual privacy and protection, ensuring that damage can be localized and managed with limited systemic repercussions.

On the other hand, blockchain technology proposes a paradigm shift towards decentralization, offering a distributed ledger system that is touted for its resistance to tampering and fraud. While blockchain can mitigate risks associated with central points of failure, it introduces new challenges. The integrity of a blockchain system is contingent on its network security. A compromise in the network could lead to broader surveillance concerns, potentially affecting multiple users at once.

The case for decentralized identity systems, such as mob.id, which employ a PKI-based structure, lies in their ability to offer a seamless and secure user experience while adhering to the rigorous standards set by ICAO and ISO. These systems leverage the established trust in PKI, while also incorporating additional layers of security and privacy, such as biometric authentication and end-to-end encryption. They provide users with control over their identity data, aligning with the European ethos of data protection and user consent.

The potential risks with a blockchain-based system primarily revolve around the immutability of the blockchain. While this feature provides security against data manipulation, it also raises concerns regarding the right to be forgotten, a cornerstone of GDPR. Solutions to this issue often involve complex off-chain storage mechanisms, which can mitigate the risk but also add layers of complexity to the system.

In conclusion, both PKI and blockchain technologies have their merits and vulnerabilities in the context of digital identity systems. The choice between them should be informed by a nuanced understanding of these factors, considering the specific application, regulatory requirements, and the overarching goal of protecting European citizens' privacy and rights. Managers must remain agile and informed, ready to adapt their strategies as technologies evolve. By prioritizing the values of privacy, consent, and security, European managers can ensure that the digital identity systems they implement serve the public good, resist unwarranted surveillance, and maintain the trust of their users.

Enhancing Data Usage Transparency in Digital Identity Systems

Transparency in the management and use of personal data is a linchpin for the credibility and success of digital identity systems in Europe. This section explores robust mechanisms and best practices for ensuring transparency, crucial for organizations to comply with stringent regulations like the GDPR and to foster trust among users.

Transparency as a Foundation for Trust

In Europe, where data protection is a right enshrined in regulation, transparency is not merely a compliance issue but a foundational element for trust in any digital identity system. This transparency involves clearly communicating how personal data is collected, used, and protected. It requires a framework where users can easily understand and manage their consent, and where they can see the audit trails of their data — who accessed it, for what purpose, and when.

Incorporating Accountability Platforms

Platforms like ArQiver, which aim to establish a "Circle of Trust" by offering transparency in information handling, embody the principles necessary for GDPR-compliant operations. Such platforms can significantly aid organizations in creating a transparent environment by providing a clear audit trail of data processing activities and enabling easy reversibility of actions when mistakes are made.

Best Practices for Enhancing Transparency

1. **Clear Communication:** Utilize tools to communicate with users about data processing activities in an understandable and accessible manner. For example, the "Privacy Nutrition Labels" concept is akin to food nutrition labels and could help distil complex data practices into simpler, standardized formats.

2. **User-Centric Data Control:** Implement systems that allow users to easily access their personal information and manage consent. This includes the ability to object to or appeal decisions made by data-processing algorithms, as well as providing clear mechanisms for data correction and deletion.

3. **Robust Audit Trails:** Maintain comprehensive records of data processing, including sources used and the purpose of processing. Platforms that help create and manage these audit trails ensure that organizations can demonstrate compliance with transparency obligations.

4. **Diverse Storage Solutions:** Employ integrated storage solutions that can work across various infrastructures, ensuring data redundancy and protection across different environments, from cloud services like Azure Blob Storage to on-premise solutions like MIN.io.

Challenges to Transparency

Implementing these transparency measures comes with its challenges, such as the complexity of data systems, the potential for information overload, and the need to balance transparency with security. Managers must navigate these challenges carefully, often requiring ongoing enhancements based on user feedback and a deep understanding of the operational domains.

Conclusion

To fulfill the promise of a transparent digital identity system that respects user privacy and complies with regulations like the GDPR, managers must adopt a multifaceted approach. This includes leveraging platforms designed to enhance accountability and using clear, user-friendly communication methods. By embedding these principles into the digital identity ecosystem, organizations can build a more trustworthy and user-empowering digital future in Europe.

Avoiding the Intensification of Socioeconomic Inequality

Introduction to the Risk of Worsening Inequality Through Digital ID Systems

The implementation of digital ID systems across Europe is poised to revolutionize how citizens interact with services and each other. Yet, within this technological leap forward lies a latent risk: the exacerbation of socioeconomic inequality.

As digital IDs become gateways to essential services, those without access or the necessary digital proficiency may find themselves further marginalized. This digital chasm, driven by unequal access to technology, threatens to deepen the divide between different social strata, potentially relegating the underprivileged to the outskirts of the digital society.

The challenge for policymakers and implementers is to navigate this transition judiciously, ensuring that digital ID systems act as equalizers rather than dividers. As Europe strides towards a digital future, it must carry forward the torch of inclusivity, illuminating the path for all its citizens, not just the digitally adept or the well-connected.

The controversy of monetizing identity data

The monetization of identity data sits at the contentious intersection of innovation and individual rights. This practice is central to the business model known as surveillance capitalism, where companies collect and analyse vast amounts of personal data to drive targeted advertising, influence consumer behaviour, and predict future actions.

Surveillance Capitalism

Shoshana Zuboff's seminal work on surveillance capitalism illuminates the underlying mechanisms where personal data becomes the raw material for commercial exploitation. In this model, data collected through digital interactions is commoditized—a trend increasingly pervasive as digital ID systems become more widespread. For example, a study in the "Harvard Business Review" revealed how companies could infer sensitive personal attributes from seemingly innocuous data points collected through digital IDs, leading to potential discrimination and privacy erosion.

Real-World Example: Social Credit Systems

A real-world manifestation of surveillance capitalism can be observed in social credit systems, such as those piloted in certain regions of China. These systems aggregate vast amounts of data from citizens' digital interactions to influence and control behaviour, often without clear consent or transparency. While such systems are not yet prevalent in Europe, the potential for similar uses of digital ID data by private entities raises ethical concerns.

Ethics of User Profiling

The ethics of user profiling come under scrutiny when considering the implications of monetizing digital ID data. The European Union's GDPR was enacted to tackle such ethical issues, mandating explicit consent and giving individuals control over their personal data. Yet, as highlighted in the European Data Protection Supervisor's (EDPS) opinions, there is a tension between the protection of personal data and the economic interests at play in surveillance capitalism.

Scholarly References

Scholarly works, such as those published in the "Journal of Business Ethics," discuss the moral imperatives in handling personal data. They argue that user profiling for profit, without robust ethical considerations, can lead to a range of harms, from identity theft to the manipulation of democratic processes. As digital ID systems gather more personal information, the scope of these risks may widen.

Case Study: The Cambridge Analytica Scandal

The Cambridge Analytica scandal serves as a cautionary tale, where data harvested from millions of individuals' digital footprints was used to influence political outcomes. This incident, examined in detail in the "Journal of Privacy and Confidentiality," underscores the dangers of unfettered access to personal data and the resultant potential for misuse.

Statistics

Statistically, the concerns are not unfounded. Reports from the Pew Research Centre show that a significant portion of the public is apprehensive about privacy and data protection, with

79% of respondents worried about the way companies are using their data.

Conclusion for Managers

For managers, the implications are clear: while digital ID systems can streamline operations and offer insights into consumer behaviour, they must navigate the ethical landscape with care. This means not only adhering to legal frameworks like the GDPR but also engaging in ethical decision-making that considers the long-term implications of data monetization. Managers must be stewards of user data, ensuring transparency, securing consent, and fostering a culture of respect for privacy that counteracts the exploitative tendencies of surveillance capitalism.

The pitfalls of mandatory enrolment in government programs

Mandatory enrolment in government digital ID programs aims to streamline services and bolster security but can also inadvertently erect barriers that reinforce and exacerbate socioeconomic disparities.

Barriers to Universal Access The push for digital IDs requires individuals to have access to digital infrastructure, which is not uniformly available across Europe. For instance, Eurostat statistics indicate that internet access in households ranges widely among EU countries, with rural and economically disadvantaged areas often lagging behind urban centres. This digital divide means that mandatory digital ID systems could exclude those without reliable internet access or the necessary devices, such as the elderly or low-income households.

Case Study: Aadhaar in India A pertinent case study is India's Aadhaar system, one of the world's largest biometric ID programs. Initially voluntary, it became quasi-mandatory for accessing various services, leading to legal challenges and public outcry. The program faced criticism when technical issues and biometric mismatches prevented individuals from receiving essential services, as documented in the "Economic & Political Weekly."

Socioeconomic Impact

The socioeconomic impact of mandatory digital ID enrolment is multifaceted. A study published in the "International Journal of Communication" highlighted that such systems could lead to a form of digital disenfranchisement for marginalized groups. In Europe, this may translate to unequal access to social benefits, healthcare, and education, essentially gatekeeping essential services based on digital proficiency and access.

Real-World Example: Estonia's Digital ID

Conversely, Estonia's digital ID system, often hailed as a model for digital governance, demonstrates how these pitfalls can be avoided. The program provides extensive access to digital services while maintaining an alternative for those not digitally enabled. Estonian authorities have actively worked to ensure widespread internet access and digital literacy, thereby minimizing the risk of socioeconomic exclusion.

Statistics and Scholarly References

The European Commission's Digital Economy and Society Index (DESI) reports disparities in digital progress among EU countries, emphasizing the need for tailored approaches to digital ID systems. Scholarly references, such as the "Journal of Information, Communication and Ethics in Society," have argued that mandatory digital ID programs must be accompanied by support systems that address the digital divide to prevent exacerbating socioeconomic inequality.

Actionable Insights for Managers

For managers, the challenge is to recognize and mitigate the risks associated with mandatory digital ID enrolment:

1. **Assess Infrastructure Readiness:** Before implementing mandatory digital ID systems, managers must evaluate whether the necessary digital infrastructure is accessible to all intended users.
2. **Provide Alternative Access Methods:** Ensure that alternative, non-digital means of accessing services are available to those who cannot or choose not to use digital IDs.
3. **Foster Digital Literacy:** Invest in educational programs that elevate the community's digital skills, making the transition to digital IDs more inclusive.
4. **Engage in Continuous Dialogue:** Maintain an open channel of communication with all stakeholders, particularly marginalized groups, to understand and address their specific challenges.

By carefully considering these factors, managers can lead the development of digital ID systems that are not only efficient and secure but also fair and inclusive, ultimately contributing to a more equitable society.

Proactive managerial strategies for equity

In the context of digital ID systems, equity is not simply a goal but a guiding principle that ensures fair access to services and opportunities across the socioeconomic spectrum. Managers, therefore, have a pivotal role in implementing proactive strategies that uphold this principle.

Supporting Not-for-Profit Identity Providers

Not-for-profit identity providers play a crucial role in creating equitable digital ID ecosystems. They are typically mission-driven, prioritizing social good over profit, and are therefore more likely to design services that are accessible and fair.

Case Study: Belgium's Citizen Cards

A case in point is the Belgian eID, a government-issued digital identity card that provides a secure method for citizens to access services and engage in e-government activities. Despite being a government initiative, it shares several not-for-profit characteristics: it prioritizes accessibility, has been incrementally funded to reduce financial barriers, and has sought to include various demographics in its design and rollout.

Real-World Example: Estonia's Digital Identity System

Estonia's digital identity system is another exemplary model. Managed by a government agency, it functions with not-for-profit principles, focusing on creating value for citizens through transparent and accessible services.

Funding and Providing Accessibility Tools

Accessibility tools are crucial in bridging the digital divide, and their provision can significantly enhance the inclusivity of digital ID systems. Funding these tools is a direct way for managers to facilitate access for all users, especially those with disabilities or limited digital literacy.

Case Study: UK's Access to Work Program

The UK's Access to Work program offers an example of how funding can be used to provide assistive technology and support for people with disabilities in the workplace. This program can be extended to include support for using digital ID systems, thereby ensuring that all citizens can participate in the digital economy.

Statistics

The European Disability Forum reports that approximately 80 million people in the EU have a disability. Ensuring that digital ID systems are accessible to this group is not only a matter of compliance with regulations such as the Web Accessibility Directive but also a moral imperative.

Facilitating Community Feedback Mechanisms

Community feedback is vital for ensuring that digital ID systems meet the needs of all users. By actively seeking and incorporating feedback, managers can ensure that these systems are user-centric and equitable.

Case Study: Aadhaar System's Community Involvement

India's Aadhaar system initially faced criticism for issues such as exclusion errors and privacy concerns. In response, the Unique Identification Authority of India (UIDAI) began to incorporate community feedback more actively, which has led to several improvements in the system.

Real-World Example: Singapore's National Digital Identity (NDI)

Program Singapore's NDI program includes a feedback mechanism that allows citizens to report issues and suggest improvements. This approach has been instrumental in refining the system to better meet the needs of a diverse user base.

Scholarly References

The concept of "co-creation" in public service design, discussed in scholarly works such as the "International Review of Administrative Sciences," emphasizes the value of involving users in the development process. This literature supports the idea that community feedback mechanisms are not just beneficial but necessary for creating equitable digital ID systems.

Actionable Insights for Managers

To operationalize these strategies, managers can take the following steps:

1. **Collaborate with Not-for-Profits:** Establish partnerships with not-for-profit organizations that have expertise in digital identity solutions to leverage their user-centric approach.
2. **Allocate Budgets for Accessibility:** Dedicate a portion of the digital ID system's budget to funding accessibility tools, ensuring that financial resources are available for this critical aspect.
3. **Incorporate Feedback into Design:** Implement systems for collecting and analysing user feedback, and establish protocols for integrating this input into the ongoing design and refinement of digital ID services.

By embedding these proactive strategies into the management of digital ID systems, managers can help mitigate the risks of inequality and ensure that the digital transformation benefits all segments of society. These efforts will contribute to a more inclusive digital future, where access to services and opportunities does not depend on one's socioeconomic status or digital proficiency.

The Road Ahead

The next chapter, "The Road Ahead," will provide a comprehensive view of the future challenges and opportunities that digital ID systems face. It will discuss the need for more balanced legislation, global standards for interoperability, and the critical importance of usability and accessibility. The chapter will also address how to focus on solutions to known barriers and the significant role ethics boards and multidisciplinary collaboration play in the evolution of digital ID systems

Introduction to the Road Ahead Chapter

Overview of the Current State of Digital ID Systems

The landscape of digital identity systems is as diverse as it is dynamic. Across the globe, nations have embarked on the journey of digitizing citizen identities, each with varying degrees of complexity and success. These systems range from India's Aadhaar, which boasts over a billion enrolled members, to Estonia's e-Residency program, renowned for its advanced e-governance services. In the European context, digital ID systems are increasingly seen as the cornerstone of digital economies, facilitating everything from banking to healthcare and voting.

The current state of these systems, however, reveals a patchwork of approaches and levels of maturity. While some countries have fully embraced digital IDs, others are still grappling with foundational challenges such as infrastructure, public trust, and legislative support. The European Union's eIDAS regulation is a significant step forward, providing a framework for mutual recognition of electronic identification across member states, but it's just the beginning. Studies show that adoption rates vary, and the full potential of these systems is yet to be realized.

The Importance of Envisioning a Roadmap for the Future

Looking ahead, the evolution of digital ID systems is not merely a technological inevitability but a strategic imperative. The future roadmap must consider not just the technological underpinnings but also the broader implications these systems have on society. This includes their impact on privacy, security, social equity, and economic participation.

A foresighted approach requires a clear vision that aligns with democratic values and human rights. For instance, scholarly work by Pohjanoksa et al. (2022) emphasizes the need for legislation that not only supports the functionality of digital IDs but also guards against abuses that could arise from their misuse. Furthermore, as Sakovich et al. (2021) argue, the future of digital identity is inherently global, necessitating standards and protocols that transcend national borders to enable interoperability and prevent digital fragmentation.

Usability and accessibility remain central to this vision, as highlighted by Preibusch (2015), who contends that the mainstream adoption of digital ID systems hinges on their ease of use and the ability to serve diverse populations, including those with disabilities or limited digital literacy. This is underscored by statistics such as those from the ITU, which indicate that while global internet penetration has grown to over 60%, disparities remain, suggesting that a significant portion of the population could be excluded from digital ID benefits.

Moreover, Cinar et al. (2019) point out that focusing on solutions to known barriers—such as digital divides, language differences, and cultural variances—is critical to the successful implementation of these systems. Ethical considerations, as Floridi (2018) articulates, must be woven into the roadmap, with ethics boards playing a pivotal role in assessing the societal impacts of digital IDs.

In summary, as we look to the road ahead, managers and policymakers must chart a course for digital ID systems that are secure, inclusive, and adaptable to future challenges. This roadmap should be built on a multi-disciplinary approach, as Mittelstadt (2019) suggests, integrating insights from law, technology, and social sciences to navigate the complex interplay between digital identities and the fabric of society.

The introduction to this chapter lays the foundation for a comprehensive exploration of the future challenges and opportunities in digital identity management. It sets the stage for a deeper dive into the legislative, technological, societal, and ethical dimensions that will shape the trajectory of digital IDs in the years to come.

The Need for Balanced Legislation and Governance Models

Discussion on the Current Legislative Landscape for Digital IDs (Pohjanoksa et al., 2022)

The legislative landscape for digital IDs is a complex and evolving field. It involves navigating the fine line between effective governance and the protection of individual rights. The European Union's eIDAS (Electronic Identification, Authentication and Trust Services) is a pioneering legislative framework that aims to standardize electronic identification and trust services for electronic transactions across EU member states. This regulation is an attempt to create a cohesive digital market and facilitate cross-border digital identification and authentication.

However, scholars like Pohjanoksa et al. (2022) emphasize that despite such frameworks, national implementations vary, leading to a fragmented digital identity landscape within the EU. The legislation, while forward-looking, must continually adapt to the rapidly advancing technological domain, addressing emerging threats and capitalizing on new opportunities. There's an ongoing discourse on how to integrate new technologies like blockchain and biometrics while safeguarding against potential risks such as surveillance and data breaches.

The Necessity for Governance Models that Balance Security, Privacy, and Accessibility

Governance models must strike a delicate balance between the competing demands of security, privacy, and accessibility. Security is paramount to protect against fraud and unauthorized access, which requires robust encryption and authentication mechanisms. At the same time, stringent security measures should not come at the expense of user privacy.

Privacy concerns in digital ID systems are manifold. They range from data misuse by third parties to government surveillance. The GDPR has set a high standard for privacy protection, but its implementation in the context of digital IDs requires careful consideration of the data minimization principle, consent mechanisms, and the right to be forgotten.

Accessibility is equally important. Digital IDs must be designed to be user-friendly and inclusive, ensuring that all citizens, irrespective of their digital literacy, can access and use these services. This involves considering language options, support for persons with disabilities, and the provision of offline alternatives or assisted services for those without reliable internet access.

Real-World Example: India's Aadhaar and the Right to Privacy

A case in point is India's Aadhaar system, which faced a significant legal challenge regarding privacy. The Supreme Court of India's landmark judgment in 2017 declared privacy a fundamental right, prompting a re-examination of Aadhaar's data collection and usage practices. The case underscores the need for governance models that robustly protect privacy even as they enable the functionality of digital IDs.

Case Study: Estonia's Digital Governance

Estonia's digital governance model is often cited as an exemplary case of balancing security and accessibility. With a high degree of transparency and citizen control over personal data, Estonia has managed to create a digital ID system that enjoys high levels of trust and participation.

Statistics and Scholarly References

Statistics show that trust in digital ID systems is highly variable across Europe. According to the Eurobarometer, trust levels can range from over 80% in some Nordic countries to below 25% in others, reflecting the diversity in public perception and the effectiveness of governance models.

Scholarly references also point to the need for dynamic governance models. Mittelstadt (2019) discusses the importance of ethics in AI and digital systems, which can be applied to digital IDs, advocating for governance models that are flexible and can evolve with technological advancements.

Actionable Insights for Managers

Managers overseeing the implementation of digital ID systems must stay informed of the evolving legislative landscape and actively participate in shaping governance models. They should:

- Engage with policymakers to advocate for laws that reflect the nuanced needs of digital ID systems.
- Implement systems that provide transparency to users about how their data is used.
- Ensure that privacy protections are baked into the design of digital IDs, in line with GDPR principles.

- Make accessibility a core consideration in the design and deployment of digital ID systems, ensuring that all citizens can benefit from the services offered.

In conclusion, balanced legislation and governance models are critical for the success of digital ID systems. They must navigate the complexities of technological innovation while upholding the fundamental values of security, privacy, and accessibility. As digital IDs become increasingly ingrained in the fabric of daily life, the responsibility to cultivate trust through balanced governance will be paramount.

The Imperative for Global Standards and Interoperability

Examination of Global Standards and Their Role in Digital ID Efficacy (Sakovich et al., 2021)

The efficacy of digital ID systems is significantly enhanced by global standards that promote interoperability. Such standards are vital for ensuring that digital identities are portable and recognized across national boundaries. Sakovich et al. (2021) discusses the International Civil Aviation Organization's (ICAO) efforts in establishing standards for machine-readable travel documents, which have been instrumental in enhancing global security and facilitating international travel. The so-called eMRTD (the ePassport or eID) is in use by more than 5.5 billion users (holders) and therefore world's largest fully decentralised Identity environment.

In the digital realm, similar standards are essential for ensuring that digital IDs can be used for a range of cross-border services, including e-commerce, finance, and e-government services. The European Union's eIDAS regulation serves as an example of an attempt to create a standardized, interoperable framework for electronic identification and trust services. However, for digital

European IDs to realize their full potential, European standards must be more widely adopted and harmonized.

Case Studies on Interoperability Protocols and Their Impact on International Cooperation

The impact of interoperability protocols on international cooperation can be observed through various case studies:

1. **Estonia and Finland Cross-Border Digital Identity**
   Estonia and Finland have implemented an interoperability protocol that allows citizens of one country to use their digital IDs to access services in the other. This cooperation has facilitated easier cross-border business and government interactions and serves as a model for the EU's broader interoperability goals.

2. **EU's STORK Project**
   The EU's STORK project aimed to establish a European eID interoperability platform that would allow citizens to use their national eIDs across EU member states. The project highlighted both the potential and the challenges of creating a pan-European digital identity ecosystem.

3. **IATA's One ID Initiative**
   The International Air Transport Association (IATA) has introduced the One ID initiative, which aims to create a seamless, contactless travel experience. By utilizing interoperable digital IDs, this initiative has the potential to streamline passenger processing and improve security in international air travel.

Statistics and Scholarly References

Statistics from the World Bank's ID4D database indicate that as of 2021, there is a growing trend towards digital ID systems, with over 60% of countries either having or developing such systems. Yet, the World Economic Forum highlights that only a fraction of these systems are designed to be interoperable at an international level.

Scholarly work in the "Journal of Global Information Technology Management" emphasizes the importance of interoperability in the global digital economy. It argues that without standardization, the potential economic benefits of digital IDs — estimated to unlock 3-13% of GDP by 2030 in the G20 countries — may not be fully realized.

Actionable Insights for Managers

For managers, the imperative for global standards and interoperability presents both a challenge and an opportunity:

Advocacy for Global Standards: Managers should engage with international bodies to advocate for the adoption of global standards for digital IDs.

Incorporation of Interoperability by Design: When developing or updating digital ID systems, include interoperability as a core design principle.

Fostering International Partnerships: Actively seek partnerships with organizations and governments to pilot cross-border digital ID initiatives.

Global standards and interoperability protocols are key enablers for the effectiveness and efficiency of digital ID systems. Managers play a crucial role in guiding the adoption and implementation of these standards to ensure that digital IDs serve as a tool for international cooperation and economic development. By focusing on interoperability, managers can contribute to a digital identity infrastructure that is robust, secure, and accessible for users across the globe.

Prioritizing Usability and Accessibility:

Crafting the Future of Digital Identity

In the digital age, identity transcends beyond the physical realm, becoming a key that unlocks a multitude of services and experiences. To turn the promise of European identity wallets into reality, the usability and accessibility of digital ID systems become paramount. They are the benchmarks that dictate how effortlessly users can interact with these systems, thus directly influencing adoption rates and the efficacy of digital IDs.

Understanding Usability and Accessibility

The success of digital IDs hinges on their design and implementation being both intuitive and accommodating. Every user, regardless of their abilities or technological expertise, must find the digital ID system approachable and manageable. As emphasized by Preibusch (2015), widespread acceptance is achieved when digital IDs are crafted with the user's experience at the forefront, ensuring that every interaction is smooth and every user feels included.

A user-centric digital ID system significantly lowers barriers, inviting adoption with open arms. Studies in the "International Journal of Human-Computer Studies" have shown that when authentication processes are streamlined without compromising security, the user experience is enriched, fostering a greater willingness to embrace digital IDs.

Illuminating Case Studies

Sweden's BankID System: This electronic identification system has earned its stripes by prioritizing user-friendly design, continually refined through user feedback and usability studies. The result? A robust system that serves as a national model for digital identification.

The UK's GOV.UK Verify: Initially, the program grappled with usability issues, which dampened adoption rates. However, a concerted effort to redesign the system for improved user-friendliness turned the tide, underscoring the critical impact of usability on user adoption.

Best Practices in Design for Digital ID Systems

To foster an environment where digital ID systems flourish, consider the following design principles:

- **Simplicity and Clarity:** Aim for a design that is straightforward and devoid of complexity. Instructions should be lucid, guiding users without reliance on technical jargon.
- **Consistency:** Employ familiar elements across the system, ensuring users are not lost in a maze of inconsistent interfaces.
- **Responsive Feedback:** Provide clear, immediate feedback during user interactions, and ensure support is readily available to address any hiccups along the way.
- **Accessibility Compliance:** Align with international accessibility standards such as WCAG to guarantee the system is inclusive for all users, regardless of their abilities.
- **Adaptive Design:** Ensure the system is responsive and adaptable to various devices to cater to the diverse preferences and circumstances of users.

Empirical Insights and Scholarly Discourse

With a billion people globally without formal IDs, the challenge to access services is not just widespread—it's a barrier to progress. The United Nations champions the cause for universal access to legal identity by 2030, emphasizing inclusivity as a pillar of sustainable development.

The "Journal of Usability Studies" and other scholarly sources affirm that a positive user experience is pivotal for the adoption of technology. Systems designed with user input are not just likely to be adopted but also used to their full potential.

A Roadmap for Managers

For managers spearheading digital ID initiatives, the path is clear:

- **User Engagement:** Involve end-users early, gathering insights into their needs to shape the system's design.
- **Usability Testing:** Conduct thorough testing at various stages, refining the system to iron out any wrinkles.
- **Educational Support:** Provide ample resources and training, supporting users as they transition to digital IDs.
- **Performance Tracking:** Keep a close watch on user satisfaction and system performance, using these metrics to steer continuous improvements.

Usability and accessibility are the twin pillars upon which successful digital ID systems stand. For managers, integrating these principles into the design process is not optional—it's a strategic imperative that paves the way for wide-scale adoption and ensures that digital ID systems truly serve as enablers of efficient and inclusive services.

Statistics and Scholarly References

According to the World Bank's Global Findex Database, as many as one billion people do not have formal IDs, which is a fundamental barrier to accessing services. Among those who do, a significant number struggle with the usability of digital systems. The United Nations emphasizes the need for inclusive identification systems, stating that ensuring universal access to legal identity by 2030 is one of its Sustainable Development Goals.

Scholarly references, such as those found in the "Journal of Usability Studies," provide evidence that user experience is a critical determinant of technology adoption. Studies have shown that systems designed with user input are more likely to be accepted and used effectively.

Addressing Barriers Beyond Identification

Exploration of Strategies to Overcome Known Barriers to Digital ID Implementation (Cinar et al., 2019)

Digital ID systems face a myriad of barriers that extend beyond the technical aspects of identification. Cinar et al. (2019) highlight those challenges such as public trust, data protection, and infrastructure limitations can impede the successful implementation of digital ID systems. They recommend a multi-faceted approach to address these barriers, emphasizing the need for clear communication, stakeholder engagement, and robust legal frameworks that safeguard privacy and security.

Strategies for Overcoming Barriers:

- **Enhancing Public Trust:** Establish clear and transparent communication channels to explain the benefits and protections of digital ID systems. For instance, Canada's Digital ID and Authentication Council of Canada (DIACC) undertakes public consultations and educational campaigns to build trust among citizens.
- **Data Protection and Privacy:** Implement privacy-by-design principles and regular audits to ensure compliance with data protection laws. The European Union's GDPR provides a strong legal framework that can be used as a benchmark for data protection in digital ID systems.

- **Infrastructure Development:** Invest in the necessary technological infrastructure to support the widespread use of digital IDs, especially in remote or underprivileged areas. Partnerships with private sector players can be instrumental in this regard, as seen in the collaboration between African governments and telecommunication companies to expand internet access.

Real-World Examples of How Proactive Solutions Can Prevent or Mitigate Issues:

Estonia's X-Road Infrastructure: Estonia's X-Road system is a stellar example of how creating a secure data exchange layer can address infrastructure challenges. It enables seamless services across various government platforms, enhancing the functionality and user experience of the Estonian digital ID ecosystem.

India's Aadhaar Enabled Payment System (AEPS): AEPS is a proactive solution to financial inclusion barriers, allowing citizens to perform financial transactions using their Aadhaar digital ID. This system has mitigated issues related to banking access in rural areas.

Statistics and Scholarly References:

According to the World Bank, approximately one billion people worldwide lack a legal ID, which is a significant barrier to accessing digital platforms. Moreover, the United Nations Sustainable Development Goal Target 16.9 aims to provide legal identity for all, including free birth registrations by 2030.

Scholarly work, such as that found in the "Journal of Identity and Migration Studies," argues that digital ID systems can significantly improve access to services if they are inclusive and account for the varying needs of diverse populations. These systems must be designed with the understanding that identification is not an end in itself but a means to access services.

Actionable Insights for Managers:

Managers must take proactive steps to address the barriers to digital ID implementation:

- **Engage** in dialogue with stakeholders, including citizens, civil society, and private sectors, to understand and address concerns related to digital IDs.
- **Collaborate** with legal experts to ensure digital ID systems comply with international data protection regulations.
- **Invest** in infrastructure that is robust and secure, prioritizing solutions that promote inclusivity and accessibility.

To realize the full potential of digital ID systems, managers must look beyond the challenges of identification and address the broader barriers that can impede implementation. By adopting proactive strategies and learning from real-world examples, managers can lead the development of digital ID systems that are inclusive, secure, and trusted by the public they aim to serve. These systems will not only provide identification but also unlock access to essential services, fostering greater social and economic inclusion.

The Role of Ethics Boards in Assessing Societal Impact

As digital ID systems become more integrated into the fabric of society, the role of ethics boards in evaluating their societal implications grows increasingly important. These boards, often composed of experts from various disciplines, provide a crucial oversight mechanism to ensure that the deployment of digital technologies aligns with societal values and ethical principles.

Function of Ethics Boards in Evaluating Digital ID Systems

Ethics boards are tasked with the responsibility of scrutinizing the moral dimensions of digital ID systems. According to Floridi (2018), these boards should not only assess compliance with current regulations but also consider broader ethical concerns such as equity, justice, and the potential for unintended consequences. For example, ethics boards can evaluate the implications of using biometric data in digital IDs, considering both the privacy risks and the potential for improved security.

Case Studies on the Impact of Ethics Boards:

The EU's Ethics Guidelines for Trustworthy AI: The European Commission's High-Level Expert Group on Artificial Intelligence developed ethics guidelines that outline seven key requirements for trustworthy AI, which are applicable to AI systems used in digital IDs. These guidelines emphasize human agency, oversight, and technical robustness, among others.

San Francisco's Banned Use of Facial Recognition: In San Francisco, ethics considerations led to the banning of the use of facial recognition technology by city agencies. The decision was influenced by an ethics board's assessment of the technology's potential for abuse and its implications for civil liberties.

Scholarly References and Statistics:

Scholarly literature, like the works published in "Ethics and Information Technology," provides a framework for understanding the role of ethics boards. These frameworks can be applied to digital ID systems to ensure that ethical deliberations are structured and thorough.

Statistics from Pew Research indicate that public concern about data privacy and surveillance is significant, with 79% of Americans concerned about how companies are using their data. This underscores the need for ethical oversight in digital ID systems, which handle sensitive personal information.

How Ethical Oversight Can Guide Responsible Development and Deployment

Ethical oversight plays a pivotal role in the responsible development and deployment of digital ID systems. It ensures that ethical considerations are not an afterthought but are integrated throughout the development process. Ethics boards can guide organizations on best practices for data minimization, consent, transparency, and the fair use of data.

Real-World Implications for Managers:

Managers involved in the deployment of digital ID systems can leverage the expertise of ethics boards to navigate complex ethical terrain. By doing so, they can:

- Ensure that digital ID systems are developed and deployed in a manner that respects user privacy and promotes fairness.
- Anticipate and mitigate potential ethical issues before they become problematic.
- Build public trust by demonstrating a commitment to ethical principles.

Ethics boards serve as a compass guiding the development and deployment of digital ID systems towards ethical north. Their role in evaluating societal implications is crucial in ensuring that these systems are not only technologically sound but also socially responsible. For managers, engaging with ethics boards is a strategic move that can help pre-emptively address ethical concerns, fostering trust and ensuring that digital ID systems are beneficial and fair for all members of society.

The Importance of Multi-Disciplinary Collaboration

The advancement of digital ID systems is not solely a technological Endeavor. It encompasses a spectrum of disciplines, including law, technology, and social sciences, each providing unique insights and tools to address the challenges posed by digital identification. As Mittelstadt (2019) suggests, the future of digital ID is contingent upon collaborative efforts that draw from the strengths of these diverse fields.

Multi-Disciplinary Collaboration to Address Future Challenges

The challenges in the digital ID space are multifaceted. Legal experts provide guidance on compliance with complex and ever-evolving data protection regulations such as the GDPR. Technologists innovate to solve problems related to security and interoperability, and social scientists study the impact of digital IDs on societal structures and individual behaviours. Only through a concerted effort can these challenges be effectively navigated.

Case Studies on Collaborative Efforts in Digital ID Systems:

Estonia's e-Governance Academy: A prime example of multidisciplinary collaboration is Estonia's e-Governance Academy, which brings together legal, technological, and policy experts to foster e-governance and digital ID solutions worldwide. The Academy has been pivotal in Estonia's success in digital governance and is now assisting other countries in developing similar frameworks.

The ID2020 Alliance: The ID2020 Alliance is a global partnership working towards providing digital IDs to the world's most vulnerable populations. The Alliance has brought together a diverse range of partners, including UN agencies, NGOs, technology companies, and academics, to develop secure, portable, and universally recognized digital ID solutions.

Statistics and Scholarly References:

Statistics from the United Nations indicate that one in seven people globally lacks a legal form of identification, which exacerbates issues of access to services and exclusion. This statistic underlines the need for holistic solutions that address both the technological aspects of digital IDs and their social implications.

Scholarly work, such as articles published in "Technology in Society," highlights the importance of interdisciplinary research in understanding the broader ramifications of technology on society. Such research provides critical insights that can guide the development of digital ID systems to ensure they are socially equitable and beneficial.

Real-World Implications for Managers:

For managers in the digital ID space, embracing multidisciplinary collaboration is essential:

- Involve legal experts early in the design process to ensure regulatory compliance and to anticipate future legal challenges.
- Partner with technologists to stay abreast of the latest advancements and to incorporate innovative solutions that enhance system security and usability.
- Engage with social scientists to understand the societal impact of digital IDs and to develop strategies that mitigate potential negative consequences.

Actionable Insights for Managers:

Managers should take proactive steps to foster multidisciplinary collaboration:

- Establish advisory boards that include legal, technological, and social science experts.

- Create platforms for dialogue and knowledge exchange among different disciplines.
- Encourage joint research and development projects that address key challenges in the digital ID space.

The successful implementation and evolution of digital ID systems hinge on a robust collaboration across multiple disciplines. Managers who understand and act upon the necessity for such interdisciplinary engagement are better equipped to navigate the complexities of digital identification. By leveraging the combined expertise of law, technology, and social sciences, digital ID systems can be crafted to meet the needs of the present while being adaptable for the challenges of the future.

Facilitating Community Feedback Mechanisms

The integration of community feedback is a critical component in the iterative process of enhancing digital ID systems. Feedback mechanisms not only provide insights into user experiences but also serve as a barometer for public sentiment and acceptance. They are essential for uncovering usability issues, gauging the effectiveness of privacy measures, and ensuring that the systems meet the diverse needs of the community.

The Role of Community Feedback in Enhancing Digital ID Systems

Community feedback plays a pivotal role in the development and refinement of digital ID systems. It helps identify pain points, areas for improvement, and user preferences. It is particularly crucial for uncovering issues that may not be apparent during the initial design and testing phases. The iterative nature of feedback loops means that digital ID systems can evolve in response to real-world use, leading to increased user satisfaction and adoption rates.

Examples of Effective Feedback Mechanisms and Their Outcomes:

Estonia's e-Residency Feedback Portal: Estonia's e-Residency program provides a digital feedback portal where users can suggest improvements, report issues, and propose new features. This input from a global user base has led to several enhancements, including the simplification of the application process and the introduction of new e-services tailored to user needs.

India's Aadhaar System Addressing Grievances: The Aadhaar system in India has implemented a comprehensive grievance redressal mechanism. It includes an online portal, a call centre, and physical centres where users can leave feedback or get assistance. This feedback system has been instrumental in addressing technical glitches and improving the user verification process.

Case Studies on the Impact of Feedback Mechanisms:

The GOV.UK Verify System: After facing initial uptake challenges, the UK government solicited user feedback through various channels, including online forums and direct outreach. The insights gained led to significant design changes that improved the system's usability and increased its adoption.

Example from the Netherlands: DigiD System Improvements

The Netherlands has a well-established digital ID system known as DigiD (Digital Identification), which allows Dutch residents to access a host of services online, from tax declarations to education and health care services. Despite its success and widespread adoption, the Dutch government has continued to seek public feedback to improve the system.

In one instance, public feedback highlighted the need for enhanced usability for elderly users and those with disabilities. The Dutch government responded by implementing a user-centred design approach, involving potential users in the design process to ensure that the system was accessible and easy to use for all demographics.

Case Study: Public Consultation for eID Framework

Additionally, the Dutch government conducted a public consultation process when developing its broader electronic identification (eID) framework, which aimed to supplement the existing DigiD system with additional means of online identification. Through this process, the government collected feedback on the proposed legislation, technical standards, and privacy implications. This consultative approach led to several iterations of the framework, with adjustments made to ensure that privacy concerns were addressed and that the eID was aligned with European standards, such as eIDAS.

The consultation process in the Netherlands demonstrates how feedback mechanisms can lead to tangible improvements in digital ID systems, ensuring they meet the needs and address the concerns of the populace. These improvements are not only technical but also policy-oriented, reflecting the multifaceted nature of digital identity management.

The Dutch example underscores the importance of community feedback mechanisms in the continuous development of digital ID systems. By prioritizing user feedback, the Netherlands has maintained a high level of public trust and satisfaction with its digital ID offerings, proving that even well-established systems can benefit from ongoing public engagement. This practice offers valuable insights for managers looking to enhance digital ID systems in their own jurisdictions.

Statistics and Scholarly References:

According to a survey by the McKinsey Global Institute, customer satisfaction can increase by 15-20% when digital ID systems are user-focused and incorporate regular feedback. Additionally, academic research published in the "Journal of Information Technology & Politics" suggests that participatory feedback mechanisms can enhance the democratic aspects of digital ID systems, leading to greater public trust and engagement.

Actionable Insights for Managers:

Managers should implement structured feedback mechanisms to capture community insights:

- Create multiple channels for feedback collection, including online platforms, social media, focus groups, and surveys.
- Analyse feedback data regularly and transparently to inform system updates and policy changes.
- Communicate changes back to the community to close the feedback loop and demonstrate responsiveness to user concerns.

In conclusion, community feedback is an invaluable resource for managers seeking to improve digital ID systems. By actively facilitating and responding to feedback, managers can ensure that digital ID systems are aligned with user needs and societal values. Such engagement not only enhances the systems themselves but also fosters a sense of ownership and trust among users, which is fundamental to the success of any digital ID initiative.

Future-Proofing Digital ID Systems

In the digital age, the agility of ID systems to adapt to both technological innovation and societal shifts is paramount. Europe, with its rich tapestry of cultures and regulations, provides a unique context for the development of digital ID systems that are robust, adaptable, and aligned with the values of its diverse population.

Strategies for Adapting to Future Technological and Societal Changes

Adaptability is the watchword for future-proofing digital ID systems. This includes creating agile frameworks that can quickly respond to emerging technologies, evolving legal landscapes, and the changing needs of society.

Modular Design: Adopting a modular approach allows for incremental updates without system-wide overhauls. The Netherlands' DigiD, for example, has evolved over time, adding new features such as DigiD Machtigen, allowing others to act on one's behalf with consent.

Open Standards: Embracing open standards, like those developed by the European Telecommunications Standards Institute (ETSI), promotes interoperability, ensuring that digital ID systems can work across borders and new platforms as they develop.

Scalability: Digital ID systems must be scalable to accommodate an increasing user base and transaction volume. The scalability of Sweden's BankID is a testament to this, allowing it to handle over 8 billion transactions annually.

Continuous Learning and Adaptation: Systems should incorporate machine learning to adapt to new fraud patterns and user behaviours. AI-driven analytics can pre-emptively identify and rectify potential security issues.

Predictions for Emerging Trends and Innovations

Europe's digital ID landscape is ripe for transformation with trends such as:

Decentralized Identity Models: Blockchain technology, particularly closed blockchain systems, is being cautiously explored for its potential in digital IDs. In my personal opinion, while blockchain offers many advantages, it's important to recognize its downsides. A closed blockchain system is advisable for government use to prevent risks like the 51% control issue. For instance, Estonia's e-governance initiative explores blockchain's utility while maintaining a closed, government-controlled system to secure digital identities.

Biometric Innovations: Countries are experimenting with new biometric technologies. Portugal's Citizen Card, for example, includes biometric data, and ongoing research is investigating even more secure biometric identifiers.

Artificial Intelligence: AI's role in automating identity verification is being piloted in various forms. France's Alicem app uses facial recognition technology to create a secure digital identity on a mobile device.

Regulatory Evolution: The EU continues to update its legal frameworks to support digital ID innovations while protecting citizens' rights, as seen in the recent proposals to update eIDAS.

Case Studies on Preparations for Technological Innovations:

Estonia's KSI Blockchain initiative illustrates the careful integration of blockchain into public digital infrastructure, enhancing the integrity of government data without exposing it to the vulnerabilities of a public blockchain.

Statistics and Scholarly References:

As reported by the European Commission, the EU's digital economy is growing rapidly, with digital ID systems being a key enabler. However, Eurostat data reveals that digital skills vary widely across the EU, highlighting the need for digital ID systems that are user-friendly and accessible to all.

Scholarly articles, such as those in the "Computer Law & Security Review," discuss the legal and technical challenges posed by blockchain in digital ID systems. They recommend closed blockchain systems for sensitive government applications to prevent issues like majority control attacks.

Actionable Insights for Managers:

Managers should focus on:

- Embracing innovation cautiously, especially with technologies like blockchain, ensuring that risks are well understood and mitigated.
- Engaging with standardization bodies to contribute to and stay informed on the latest developments in digital ID standards.
- Investing in technologies that enhance the security and usability of digital ID systems while safeguarding user privacy.

Future-proofing digital ID systems in Europe requires a strategic blend of innovation, adaptability, and precaution. By prioritizing scalability, interoperability, and user-centric design, and by approaching emerging technologies like blockchain with a critical yet open mindset, European managers can lead the development of digital ID systems that are secure, efficient, and respectful of the rich societal values across the continent.

In the pursuit of resilient digital ID systems, Europe's approach has been characterized by a blend of innovation and reliance on proven technologies. Among these, Public Key Infrastructure (PKI) has been a cornerstone for securing digital transactions and identities for several years.

The Role of PKI in Decentralized Identities

PKI presents a mature, tested framework for managing digital identities in a decentralized manner. It provides mechanisms for individuals and entities to securely communicate and transact online through the use of public and private cryptographic keys, which are issued by trusted Certificate Authorities (CAs).

- **Proven System:** Unlike the relatively nascent blockchain technology, PKI has been in use for decades, providing a reliable method for authenticating and encrypting data. For example, the Estonian e-ID utilizes PKI to secure its digital identities, allowing for secure electronic communications and transactions across the country.
- **Performance Efficiency:** PKI systems, by their nature, do not suffer from the performance issues often associated with blockchain, such as slow transaction times during periods of high demand. They are optimized for quick and secure verification processes, essential for user acceptance and system reliability.
- **Fully Decentralized and Low Risk:** PKI allows for a fully decentralized system, where identities are not reliant on a single point of control, thereby reducing the risk of systemic failure. The decentralization in PKI is about the distribution of trust rather than the distribution of ledger entries, as is the case with blockchain. This approach significantly lowers the risk associated with centralized data storage and management.

Statistics and Scholarly References:

The robustness of PKI is supported by its extensive adoption across various sectors. A report by the GlobalSign PKI survey found that 60% of organizations use PKI credentials for internal users, which speaks to its trusted status. Scholarly references, like those in the "Journal of Network and Computer Applications," praise PKI for its ability to secure communications in a wide array of environments, from mobile to cloud services.

Actionable Insights for Managers:

For managers, incorporating PKI into digital ID systems means leveraging a time-tested, efficient, and secure framework. They should:

- Ensure the selection of reputable CAs to underpin the trust model of their PKI system.
- Regularly update and manage the lifecycle of digital certificates to maintain system integrity.
- Educate users on the importance and benefits of PKI in protecting their digital identities.

As we look towards future-proofing digital ID systems, the integration of PKI stands out as a practical and prudent step. Its proven track record, efficiency, and low-risk profile in managing decentralized identities make it an indispensable component of any comprehensive digital ID strategy. By building upon the solid foundation provided by PKI, European digital ID systems can continue to evolve while ensuring the security and trust of their users.

Policy Recommendations and Managerial Implications

Comprehensive Policy Recommendations for Future Digital ID Governance

As Europe continues to navigate the complex landscape of digital identification, policymakers play a crucial role in shaping the future of digital ID governance. Drawing from the lessons learned and best practices established across the continent, the following are comprehensive policy recommendations:

- **Emphasize Privacy and Security:** Policies should reinforce privacy by design and default, as mandated by the GDPR. This ensures that digital ID systems are secure and that personal data is protected from the outset. For instance, Germany's Federal Data Protection Act provides a robust framework that other countries could emulate.

- **Ensure Interoperability and Standards Compliance:** Adopt international standards like ISO/IEC 27001 for information security management to facilitate interoperability across borders. The European Union's eIDAS regulation serves as a model for standardizing electronic identification and trust services.

- **Promote Inclusivity and Accessibility:** Governance policies must mandate that digital ID systems are accessible to all citizens, including those with disabilities and those without access to technology. The EU Web Accessibility Directive is an important step in this direction.

- **Foster Public Trust through Transparency:** Transparency in how digital ID systems operate and how data is used can build public trust. The EU's transparency framework for public services could provide a template for digital ID systems.

Case Studies on Policy Impact:

Estonia's Digital Identity Framework: Estonia has enacted policies that have made it a leader in digital governance, with its digital ID system being a prime example of public trust and widespread usage.

Denmark's NemID and its Transition to MitID: Denmark's NemID system has set policies in place for a smooth transition to the newer MitID system, with emphasis on maintaining user trust and security during the changeover.

Statistics and Scholarly References:

According to Eurostat, 90% of Europeans expect to use some form of online identity verification by 2030. Scholarly work by authors such as Kubicek and Noack (2010) in "Government Information Quarterly" discusses the need for governance frameworks that can keep pace with such rapid adoption.

Implications for Managers Overseeing the Implementation of Digital ID Systems

For managers, the implications of these policy recommendations are multifaceted:

- **Strategic Planning:** Managers must align digital ID system development with long-term policy goals, ensuring systems are built to last and adapt to regulatory changes.
- **Stakeholder Engagement:** Actively engage with stakeholders, including legal experts, technologists, and end-users, to understand their needs and concerns.
- **Continuous Improvement:** Stay informed about technological advancements and policy shifts to keep digital ID systems current and compliant.
- **Risk Management:** Develop strategies for risk assessment and mitigation, especially in relation to data breaches and privacy concerns.

Actionable Insights for Managers:

Managers should take proactive steps, such as:

- Establishing clear governance structures for digital ID systems within their organizations.
- Creating mechanisms for regular review and updating of digital ID policies to reflect new legal and technological developments.
- Training staff on the implications of digital ID policies and the importance of compliance.

The future of digital ID governance in Europe requires a delicate balance between technological advancement, regulatory compliance, and the management of complex systems. Policies need to be forward-looking and adaptable, while managers must be vigilant and proactive in their implementation. The successful governance of digital IDs hinges on an informed and strategic approach that anticipates future trends and addresses the evolving needs of society.

Conclusion

As we conclude our exploration of the multifaceted digital ID landscape, it's clear that these systems stand at the crossroads of technology, policy, and society. The future of digital ID systems is not merely contingent upon the sophistication of their technological underpinnings but also on how they are governed, perceived, and integrated into the daily lives of citizens.

Synthesis of Discussed Topics and Their Significance

The discussed topics have illustrated that digital ID systems are a nexus of innovation and regulation. From the robust legal frameworks that ensure privacy and security to the technological advancements that promise enhanced usability and accessibility, digital ID systems are being shaped by a diverse array of forces.

The significance of these systems lies in their potential to transform how we engage with services, conduct transactions, and prove our identities. Yet, with great potential comes great responsibility. As the case studies from Estonia and the Netherlands have shown, careful planning, public trust, and an inclusive approach are critical for the successful adoption of digital ID systems.

Statistics and Scholarly References

Statistical evidence supports the importance of these systems. According to the European Commission's Digital Economy and Society Index (DESI), Europe has seen consistent growth in the integration of digital technologies, with digital IDs being a significant contributor to this trend. Scholarly works, like those of Mayer-Schönberger and Cukier in "Big Data: A Revolution That Will Transform How We Live, Work, and Think," emphasize the transformative power of digital data management — of which digital IDs are a crucial component.

The Collective Effort in Navigating the Digital Landscape

Navigating the evolving digital landscape requires a concerted and collective effort from policymakers, technologists, managers, and society at large. The interplay between these actors determines the trajectory of digital ID systems. Policymakers must craft regulations that protect citizens while fostering innovation. Technologists must design systems that prioritize user needs and adaptability. Managers must implement these systems in ways that align with both regulatory requirements and the expectations of users.

Actionable Insights for Managers

In light of these discussions, managers should take away a few key insights:

- Stay abreast of legislative changes and technological trends to ensure digital ID systems remain compliant and relevant.
- Foster an organizational culture that values user privacy, security, and inclusivity.
- Engage in continuous dialogue with stakeholders to maintain public trust and encourage widespread adoption.

Final Thoughts

The future of digital ID systems is not preordained; it will be written by the actions we take today. By acknowledging the complexity of the digital ID ecosystem and embracing a holistic approach to its development and governance, we can build systems that are not only efficient and secure but also equitable and trusted. The collective effort to achieve this goal will be the defining factor in how digital ID systems shape our digital future. As we look ahead, it is this collaborative spirit that will enable us to navigate the digital landscape with confidence and optimism.

Implementing an ICAM project using mob.id

Executive Summary

Project Overview and Strategic Importance

This project aims to overhaul the current identity and access management (IAM) framework of a large government organization by implementing mob.id in conjunction with viewDS and promoting it to a fine-grained and high secure Identity, Credential Access Management (ICAM). The strategic importance of this initiative cannot be overstated; it represents a fundamental shift towards a more modern, secure, and flexible ICAM solution that is crucial for national security, data protection, and operational efficiency.

The current reliance on traditional Active Directory (AD) systems presents multiple challenges in the face of evolving cybersecurity threats. This project will replace the AD infrastructure, addressing its limitations with a robust system that offers enhanced security measures, including a Public Key Infrastructure (PKI) based Identity for multi-factor zero knowledge Identification and a comprehensive Identity, Credential, and Access Management (ICAM) strategy.

Identity and Access Management (IAM) systems like Active Directory (AD) typically provide basic functions such as maintaining user profiles, authentication, and authorization within an organization. They are often centralized and can be limited in scalability and flexibility, particularly in complex environments with high-security demands. IAM focuses on ensuring that the right individuals access the right resources at the right times for the right reasons, but it may not always provide the granularity and control required for highly secure or zero-trust environments.

Identity, Credential and Access Management (ICAM), on the other hand, is a more comprehensive approach that encompasses IAM and extends it with additional layers of security. ICAM systems like with mob.id and ViewDS offer a holistic solution by not only managing identities and access but also by incorporating credential management, which involves issuing, renewing, and revoking credentials based on predefined policies. This allows for a more nuanced approach to security, enabling multifactor authentication (MFA), role-based access control (RBAC), and attribute-based access control (ABAC), which are integral to a zero-trust security model.

ICAM is crucial for a zero-trust architecture, which operates on the principle of "never trust, always verify." It assumes that threats can exist both outside and inside the network, and therefore, no users or systems should be inherently trusted. Instead, trust levels are dynamically assigned based on identity verification, context, and risk assessment, with security enforced at multiple levels. ICAM facilitates this by allowing different levels of credentials and access permissions, enabling organizations to enforce strict access controls and policies that adapt to real-time risk assessments, ensuring that users have access only to the resources necessary for their **role AND current context**. This granularity and adaptability make ICAM systems like mob.id with ViewDS indispensable for organizations that require stringent security measures and operate under a zero-trust security framework.

Alignment with Organizational Security Requirements

The existing AD system, while foundational to the organization's operations, has become increasingly misaligned with the stringent security requirements necessary for government functions. The introduction of mob.id, supplemented by viewDS, aligns with the organization's need for a high-assurance identity system that can mitigate risks associated with credential management and access control.

The proposed solution will meet and exceed current security standards by incorporating strong authentication mechanisms, advanced credentialing processes, and seamless access control, all while ensuring compliance with European Union regulations and standards, including GDPR and eIDAS.

Benefits of Transitioning to mob.id with viewDS from Active Directory

Transitioning to mob.id with viewDS offers several key benefits over the existing AD system:

- **Enhanced Security:** Mob.id with viewDS provides a multi-layered security approach that leverages PKI technology, reducing the risk of data breaches and unauthorized access.
- **Greater Flexibility:** Unlike AD, which can be rigid in its structure, mob.id offers a flexible and modular approach to identity management, capable of adapting to emerging technologies and changing organizational needs.
- **Improved User Experience:** The user experience will be significantly enhanced, with streamlined access to services and a reduction in authentication complexities, particularly for mobile and remote access.
- **Reduced Operational Strain:** By addressing the performance issues and help desk pressures associated with AD, the new system will alleviate operational burdens, leading to increased efficiency and user satisfaction.
- **Increased Accountability:** The integration of viewDS will provide better audit trails and reporting capabilities,

leading to increased transparency and accountability within the organization's IAM processes.

In summary, the executive summary outlines the urgent need for an updated IAM system, the alignment of the proposed solution with the organization's security requirements, and the multitude of benefits that mob.id with viewDS as a complete ICAM offers. It sets the stage for a comprehensive project plan that will detail the transition away from AD towards a future-proofed IAM infrastructure.

Project Objectives and Scope

Defining the Project's Main Goals

The primary goals of this project are threefold, each critical to the overarching mission of the organization's digital transformation:

1. **Security Enhancement:**
    a. Implement state-of-the-art security protocols using mob.id, which integrates PKI for robust authentication, enhancing the overall security posture and reducing the risk of identity-related breaches.
    b. Ensure that all digital identity interactions across the organization are secure, auditable, and compliant with European Union privacy and security standards.
2. **System Integration:**
    a. Seamlessly integrate mob.id with viewDS to create a cohesive ICAM system that works in concert with existing enterprise applications and databases.
    b. Establish a unified platform for identity management that facilitates real-time

synchronization and coordination across various organizational systems and services.

3. **User Experience:**
   a. Deliver a streamlined and intuitive user experience for both administrative staff and end-users, minimizing complexity and enhancing productivity.
   b. Develop a user-friendly interface that simplifies credential management and access control processes, reducing the need for help desk support and user training.

Outlining the Scope

The scope of this project encompasses several key components and considerations:

1. **System Components:**
   - Deployment of mob.id services as a cloud-based solution, removing the dependency on local infrastructure and enabling scalable, flexible identity management.
   - Implementation of viewDS as the directory system, providing a rich feature set for identity data storage, retrieval, and synchronization.
   - Integration of PKI-based authentication tokens, offering a higher level of security for accessing sensitive information and services.

2. **User Groups:**
   - Inclusion of all current AD user accounts, spanning across various departments and levels of access requirements, from regular staff to high-privilege users.
   - Consideration of external stakeholders who require access to the organization's systems,

ensuring they are also transitioned to the new ICAM framework.

3. **Data Migration:**
   - A comprehensive plan for migrating existing identity data from AD to the new mob.id and viewDS system, ensuring data integrity and minimal service disruption.
   - Strategies for archiving historical data and providing continuity of access where necessary.

4. **Implementation Phases:**
   - A phased rollout that begins with a pilot program, followed by a department-by-department transition, concluding with a full organizational switch-over.
   - Detailed timelines for each phase, including milestones for the integration of different system components and user groups.

5. **Training and Support:**
   - Development of training programs tailored to various user groups, ensuring a smooth transition to the new system.
   - Establishment of a dedicated support team to assist with the migration and to address any issues that arise during and after the rollout.

6. **Post-Implementation Review:**
   - A structured plan for reviewing the success of the implementation, measuring system performance, user satisfaction, and security efficacy.

The objectives and scope of this project are designed to transition the organization to a cutting-edge ICAM solution that prioritizes security, integration, and a superior user experience. This phase of the project plan sets clear, measurable goals and outlines the breadth of work required to achieve a successful transformation in the organization's identity management practices.

Current System Analysis

Evaluation of the Existing Active Directory Setup

The existing Active Directory (AD) setup functions as the central pillar for managing user identities and access within the organization. It has been the traditional go-to IAM solution, enabling domain-based network management and streamlined user administration. However, an in-depth evaluation reveals several areas where the AD infrastructure might fall short in the current high-security demand landscape.

Identification of Security Limitations and Operational Pressures

- Single Point of Failure: As a centralized system, AD can be a single point of failure, making it vulnerable to targeted cyber-attacks which, if successful, could compromise the entire network.
- Limited Flexibility: AD's rigid hierarchical structure often impedes rapid adjustments to access controls, which is crucial in a dynamic security environment.
- Scalability Issues: As the organization grows and the number of users and devices increases, AD may struggle to manage the scale efficiently, leading to performance bottlenecks.

Operational Pressures on CISO and Help Desk:

- The CISO faces increased pressure to maintain a secure environment as threat vectors evolve, and AD's limited capability to enforce advanced security policies, such as zero-trust principles, becomes a concern.

- The help desk experiences high volumes of service requests related to password resets and access issues, indicative of the need for a more user-friendly and autonomous system.

Impact of Current System Limitations on Organizational Security Posture

The limitations of the current AD setup have several implications for the organization's overall security posture:

- **Security Risks:** Inability to swiftly adapt to new security threats leaves the organization at risk of data breaches and unauthorized access to sensitive information.
- **Compliance Challenges:** Compliance with stringent regulatory standards like GDPR may be compromised if the system cannot enforce the necessary controls over personal data access and processing.
- **User Productivity:** Inefficiencies in the system can lead to increased downtime and frustration for users, directly impacting productivity and job satisfaction.
- **Strain on Resources:** The current setup may require more manual interventions and oversight, placing a strain on IT resources and potentially increasing operational costs.

Conclusion and Next Steps

The evaluation underlines the need for an overhaul of the current IAM approach. The organization must transition to a more robust, flexible, and scalable ICAM solution that can meet the demands of a high-security, zero-trust architecture. The next steps involve defining a clear strategy to address these issues, considering the integration of advanced solutions like mob.id and viewDS, which can provide a more secure, agile, and user-friendly identity management environment. This will form the basis of a detailed project plan aimed at strengthening the organization's security infrastructure while alleviating operational pressures.

Solution Overview

The planned upgrade to the organization's identity management system necessitates a comprehensive solution that not only addresses current shortcomings but also positions us for future challenges and innovations. The proposed integration of mob.id and viewDS represents a holistic approach to identity, credential, and access management (ICAM), tailored to meet the stringent security requirements and operational demands of our organization.

Introduction to mob.id and viewDS as an Integrated ICAM Solution

Mob.id serves as a modern identity wallet, harnessing the robust standards of ICAO and ISO to offer a secure, mobile-centric approach to identity management. Its unique capability to store various digital credentials and convert unsecured smartphones into trusted devices makes it a versatile tool for identity verification across ICAO's member countries.

ViewDS complements mob.id by providing a comprehensive directory system that includes advanced identity data storage, retrieval, and synchronization. When combined, mob.id and viewDS create an integrated ICAM framework that facilitates a more nuanced, secure, and user-centric identity management experience. This integration aligns with the principles of a zero-trust architecture, ensuring that access to organizational resources is continuously verified and only granted when necessary and justified.

Benefits of Using mob.id and viewDS for Enhanced Security and Efficiency

The transition to mob.id with viewDS offers numerous benefits:

- **Advanced Security Features:** The integration leverages PKI and multi-factor authentication mechanisms, significantly enhancing the security of digital identities and reducing the potential for unauthorized access.
- **Operational Efficiency:** With viewDS, identity information is managed more effectively, reducing the administrative burden on IT staff and streamlining user access processes.
- **Improved Compliance:** The solution is designed with GDPR and eIDAS in mind, ensuring compliance with European data protection and digital identity standards.
- **Scalability and Flexibility:** The cloud-based nature of mob.id and the adaptable infrastructure of viewDS provide scalability to accommodate organizational growth and the flexibility to integrate with future technologies.

Comparison with Active Directory and Justification for Transition

While Active Directory has been the foundational IAM tool for many organizations, its limitations in a high-security environment have become apparent. In comparison, mob.id and viewDS offer:

- **Decentralized Identity Management:** Unlike AD's centralized model, mob.id and viewDS allow for a decentralized approach, mitigating the risks associated with a single point of failure.
- **Enhanced Access Management:** The ICAM solution provides granular access controls that can be dynamically adjusted, aligning with zero-trust security principles.

- **Reduced Help Desk Workload:** With self-service options and simplified credential management, mob.id reduces the reliance on help desk support for routine tasks such as password resets.

Future-Readiness: Mob.id and viewDS are built to accommodate emerging technologies and security protocols, making them more sustainable solutions in the long term.

The solution overview presents a compelling case for adopting mob.id and viewDS as an integrated ICAM system. This transition not only addresses the immediate need for enhanced security and operational efficiency but also provides a scalable and flexible platform for the organization's future identity management needs. The benefits of this solution, when compared to the limitations of Active Directory, provide clear justification for the transition and set the stage for a detailed plan of implementation.

Project Requirements

For the successful implementation of an Integrated Credential and Access Management (ICAM) system using mob.id and viewDS, it is essential to delineate the project requirements clearly. These requirements form the blueprint for the project's success and ensure that the solution aligns with organizational goals, legal standards, and user needs.

Detailed Requirements for ICAM System Implementation

Functional Requirements:

- The system must support PKI-based identity verification for privileged users and two-factor authentication for general access.
- It should provide role-based and attribute-based access controls that can be dynamically adjusted in real-time.

- The system must be capable of integrating with existing enterprise applications and databases.
- It should offer a user-friendly interface for credential management, accessible via mobile and desktop platforms.
- The system must provide robust logging and audit trails for all user activities and access changes.

Technical Requirements:

- The solution must be scalable to handle an increasing number of users and transactions.
- It must ensure high availability and disaster recovery capabilities.
- The system should be compatible with European digital identity frameworks and support cross-border operations.
- It must include comprehensive data migration tools for transitioning from Active Directory to the new ICAM system.

Performance Requirements:

- The ICAM system should meet predefined performance benchmarks, including response times and transaction processing speeds.
- It must be resilient to high traffic loads and provide consistent performance even during peak usage.

Legal and Regulatory Compliance Checkpoints

GDPR Compliance:

- The system must incorporate data protection by design and by default, offering data minimization and pseudonymization where feasible.

- It must provide users with the ability to access, rectify, and erase their personal data in compliance with GDPR 'right to be forgotten' stipulations.

eIDAS Alignment:

- The ICAM system should adhere to eIDAS regulations for electronic identification and trust services, ensuring that digital credentials are EU-wide recognized.
- It must support the issuance, validation, and revocation of electronic signatures and seals.

National Regulations:

The system should comply with any relevant national laws governing digital identity and cybersecurity, which may vary from country to country within the EU.

User Requirements and Security Considerations

1. **User-Centric Design:**
   - The ICAM system should cater to a diverse user base, with customization options to accommodate individual user preferences and needs.
   - It must prioritize ease of use to minimize the learning curve and encourage user adoption.
2. **Security Protocols:**
   - The system must implement the latest encryption standards to protect data at rest and in transit.
   - It should be capable of detecting and responding to security incidents swiftly and effectively.
   - The system must enforce strict password policies and account management practices to protect against unauthorized access.
3. **Zero-Trust Framework:**

- The ICAM system must be designed around a zero-trust model, requiring continuous verification of all users and devices.
- It should enforce least-privilege access, ensuring users have only the necessary permissions to perform their tasks.

Setting forth these detailed project requirements is a critical step in ensuring the successful deployment of the ICAM system. They provide a comprehensive framework that will guide the selection of features, the design of user interfaces, the integration with existing systems, and the adherence to legal and security standards. This approach underscores the commitment to delivering a secure, efficient, and user-friendly identity management solution that aligns with both the strategic goals of the organization and the stringent regulations governing digital identity in Europe.

VI. Project Team and Governance

For a project of this magnitude, establishing a clear governance structure is essential for smooth execution and successful delivery. This involves defining roles and responsibilities, setting up decision-making frameworks, and creating efficient collaboration and reporting channels.

Defining Project Roles and Responsibilities

- **Project Sponsor:** Typically, a senior executive who champions the project at the highest level, ensuring it aligns with strategic objectives and secures necessary resources.
- **Project Manager:** Responsible for day-to-day management, coordinating teams, maintaining timelines, and ensuring that project milestones are met.

- **Technical Lead:** Oversees the technical aspects of the project, from architecture design to deployment, ensuring that technical requirements are fulfilled.
- **Security and Compliance Officer:** Ensures that the project meets all security standards and legal requirements, and is responsible for managing risks related to cybersecurity and data protection.
- **Change Management Lead:** Focuses on managing organizational change associated with the project, including training programs and user onboarding.
- **Quality Assurance Manager:** Ensures that the project's deliverables meet quality standards and that testing protocols are followed.
- **Support and Maintenance Lead:** Develops the support structure for the post-deployment phase and oversees the maintenance of the new system.
- **User Experience (UX) Designer:** Ensures that the system is user-friendly and that the design facilitates ease of use and satisfaction.
- **Business Analyst:** Gathers and analyzes business requirements to ensure that the system aligns with organizational workflows and user needs.
- **IT Support Staff:** Provides technical support during and after the implementation, assisting users with the new system.
- **Training Coordinator:** Develops training materials and coordinates training sessions for users and IT staff.

Establishing Governance Structure for Decision-Making and Oversight

- **Steering Committee:** Comprising senior stakeholders, this group makes strategic decisions, resolves high-level issues, and provides direction and oversight.

- **Technical Advisory Group:** A panel of technical experts that advises on technology choices, integration challenges, and future-proofing the system.
- **Project Management Office (PMO):** Acts as the central hub for project documentation, tracking, and reporting, ensuring consistency and alignment with the project plan.

Outlining Collaboration and Reporting Mechanisms

- **Regular Status Meetings:** Scheduled meetings with key project members to discuss progress, challenges, and next steps.
- **Collaborative Tools:** Utilization of project management software and collaboration platforms to maintain communication among team members and stakeholders.
- **Reporting Structure:** A standardized reporting format for project updates, risk assessments, and compliance checks to be shared with the steering committee and other relevant parties.
- **Feedback Loops:** Mechanisms to gather feedback from stakeholders and end-users to inform decision-making and project adjustments.
- **Escalation Procedures:** Clearly defined protocols for escalating issues that cannot be resolved at lower levels of the project team structure.

A well-defined project team and governance structure are the backbones of any successful project. For the implementation of mob.id with viewDS, it is critical to establish clear roles, a decision-making hierarchy, and effective collaboration practices. This ensures that the project remains on track, decisions are made efficiently, and all team members are aligned with the project's goals and objectives. By adhering to these governance principles, the organization can confidently navigate the complexities of upgrading its digital identity management system.

Implementation Strategy

The implementation strategy is a critical roadmap for integrating the new ICAM system with minimal disruption. It will be a phased, systematic process, ensuring each stage is managed effectively with clear objectives and review points.

Phased Approach to System Integration and User Migration

1. **Pilot Phase:**
   - Select a small, controlled user group to implement the initial rollout of mob.id and viewDS.
   - Gather data on system performance and user feedback to refine the implementation process.
2. **Departmental Rollout:**
   - Expand the rollout to include entire departments, one at a time, allowing for focused support and troubleshooting.
   - Use lessons learned from the pilot phase to streamline the migration process.
3. **Organizational Adoption:**
   - After successful departmental integrations, proceed with organization-wide adoption.
   - Ensure robust training and support structures are in place for all users.
4. **Post-Integration Review:**
   - Conduct thorough reviews after each phase to assess if the project is meeting defined milestones and objectives.
   - Adjust the rollout plan based on these reviews to address any issues.

Strategy for PKI-Based Identity Wallet Rollout for Sensitive Information Access

1. **Credential Issuance:**
   - Develop a secure process for issuing PKI-based tokens to authorized personnel, ensuring that tokens are distributed in a controlled manner.
   - Integrate the token issuance process with mob.id for seamless credential management.

2. **Access Control Update:**
   - Update access control policies to require PKI-based identities for sensitive systems, ensuring that all privileged actions are secured.
   - Provide training for users on the new access control measures to ensure a smooth transition.

3. **Monitoring and Revocation:**
   - Implement monitoring systems to track token usage and detect any anomalies.
   - Establish a clear procedure for identity revocation and reissuance in case of security incidents or identity expiry.

Continuity Plans for Maintaining Service Availability During Transition

1. **Redundancy Measures:** Ensure that critical systems have redundancy in place to maintain service availability if the new ICAM system encounters issues during the transition.

2. **Rollback Procedures:** Develop and test rollback procedures to revert to the previous system if a critical failure occurs with the new ICAM system.

3. **Communication Protocols:** Establish clear communication channels to inform users of system

status and provide guidance during the transition period.

The implementation strategy for mob.id with viewDS must be methodical and flexible. By adopting a phased approach, the organization can ensure that each stage of the migration is handled with due diligence, providing ample opportunity for adjustment and improvement. The careful rollout of PKI-based identities will enhance the security of sensitive information, and continuity plans will safeguard service availability, ensuring that the organization remains operational and secure throughout the transition. This strategic approach lays the groundwork for a successful digital transformation, reinforcing the organization's commitment to security and efficiency

Technical Architecture and Design

The technical architecture and design of the integrated mob.id and viewDS solution are critical to achieving a secure and seamless identity management system. This section will outline the architecture, the data migration strategy from Active Directory, and the security measures that will be implemented, with a focus on the PKI-based identity wallet aspect of mob.id.

Detailed Architecture of the Integrated mob.id and ViewDS Solution

1. **Infrastructure Overview:**
   - The architecture will be based on a distributed model where mob.id acts as a PKI-based identity wallet, enabling secure storage and management of identity credentials on users' devices.
   - ViewDS will serve as the authoritative source of identity data, with a synchronization mechanism to ensure consistency between the identity wallet and the central directory.

2. **Service Components:**
   - The mob.id service will include identity enrollment and credential issuance services, authentication services, and an administration console for managing identity verification workflows.
   - ViewDS will be configured to handle identity data management, including user attributes and access controls, with real-time replication and backup for disaster recovery.

3. **Integration Layer:**
   - A secure API layer will facilitate communication between mob.id, viewDS, and other organizational systems, ensuring that data flows are encrypted and authenticated.

Data Migration Strategy from Active Directory

1. **Data Assessment and Cleansing:**
   - A thorough review of the current Active Directory schema will be conducted to identify all data elements for migration to viewDS.
   - Data cleansing processes will be put in place to ensure that only accurate, up-to-date, and necessary data is migrated, adhering to the principles of data minimization.

2. **Migration Execution:**
   - The migration will occur in a phased approach, starting with non-sensitive information and gradually moving to more critical data.
   - A rollback strategy will be prepared in case any step of the migration process encounters issues.

3. **Verification and Auditing:**
   - Post-migration, the data will be audited for integrity and completeness against predefined verification criteria.

- Users will verify their information post-migration through the mob.id app, ensuring that their PKI-based identity wallet contains the correct credentials.

Security Measures, Including PKI Token Implementation

1. **PKI Infrastructure:**
   - mob.id will utilize a robust PKI infrastructure to issue identities protected with digital certificates that will be stored securely on users' devices, enabling strong identity verification combined with liveness detection.
   - The PKI system is designed with high availability and redundancy to ensure uninterrupted identity and certificate issuance and validation services.

2. **Access Control and Identity Management:**
   - Access to sensitive information and systems will require strong multi-factor identification, utilizing mob.id identities.
   - Fine-grained Attribute Based Access Control Policy-based access controls will be configured in viewDS, with rules that specify the required level of verification for different types of resources.

3. **Continuous Security Monitoring:**
   - Continuous monitoring solutions will be put in place to track access and authentication attempts, flagging any anomalous activities for immediate investigation.
   - Regular security assessments will be conducted to ensure the ICAM system adheres to evolving security best practices and threat landscapes.

The technical architecture and design of the mob.id and viewDS solution will establish a robust, PKI-based identity management framework that enhances the security and efficiency of the organization's operations. The strategic migration from Active Directory to this new system will be executed with precision to ensure data integrity and system reliability. Security is paramount in this design, with a PKI infrastructure at the core, providing a strong foundation for secure digital interactions and access management within the organization.

Risk Management Plan

A robust Risk Management Plan is essential to pre-emptively address and mitigate potential risks associated with the implementation of the mob.id and viewDS solution. This plan will outline the risk identification process, propose mitigation strategies, address security-specific risks with contingencies, and tackle user adoption risks through change management strategies.

Identification of Potential Risks and Mitigation Strategies

1. System Integration Complexity:
   - **Risk:** Integration with existing IT infrastructure may encounter unforeseen complexities, leading to project delays.
   - **Mitigation:** Engage experienced integration specialists early and conduct a thorough system requirements analysis. Use a sandbox environment for testing integration points before live deployment.
2. Data Integrity During Migration:
   - **Risk:** Potential for data corruption or loss during the migration from Active Directory to mob.id with viewDS.
   - **Mitigation:** Implement a comprehensive data backup plan. Migrate data in stages and validate each stage for accuracy before proceeding.

3. Budget Overruns and Resource Allocation:
- **Risk:** The project could exceed the budget or suffer from misallocated resources.
- **Mitigation:** Use project management software to track expenditures and resource usage in real-time. Regularly review the budget against project milestones.

Security-Specific Risks and Contingencies

1. **Security Breaches During Transition:**
   - Risk: Increased vulnerability to cyber attacks during the switch-over to the new system.
   - Mitigation: Establish a cybersecurity task force to monitor the transition process. Utilize encryption and conduct penetration testing to fortify security before going live.
2. **Identity Distribution and Management:**
   - Risk: PKI tokens, if not managed correctly, could be lost, stolen, or misused, resulting in unauthorized access.
   - Mitigation: Develop strict protocols for PKI token issuance and revocation. Employ multi-factor authentication and educate users on securing their tokens.
3. **Compliance with Data Protection Regulations:**
   - Risk: New system features or processes could inadvertently violate GDPR or other privacy laws.
   - Mitigation: Involve compliance officers in the design phase and conduct regular compliance audits. Implement features such as consent management and data minimization.

User Adoption Risks and Change Management

1. **Resistance to Change:**

- **Risk:** Users may be resistant to learning a new system, leading to a slow adoption rate.
- **Mitigation:** Develop a change management plan that includes communication strategies, user involvement in the design and testing phases, and visible endorsement from leadership.

2. **Training and Support Challenges:**
   - **Risk:** Inadequate training could lead to confusion and inefficiency, placing additional strain on support services.
   - **Mitigation:** Create comprehensive training programs, supplemented with e-learning modules and quick-reference guides. Establish a help desk specifically for the transition period.

3. **Monitoring Adoption Rates:**
   - **Risk:** Failure to accurately monitor adoption rates could mask underlying issues with the new system.
   - **Mitigation:** Set clear KPIs for adoption and usage. Utilize surveys and feedback tools to gather user feedback and make necessary adjustments.

The Risk Management Plan is a foundational component that ensures the project's integrity and success. By identifying potential risks and establishing detailed mitigation strategies, the organization can maintain control over the project's trajectory. Security risks require vigilant attention, particularly when implementing PKI-based solutions that are integral to the system's trust architecture. Finally, addressing user adoption through comprehensive change management initiatives will facilitate a smoother transition and foster a positive reception of the new ICAM system.

Training and Communication Plan

A well-articulated Training and Communication Plan is essential for the successful implementation of the mob.id and viewDS solution. This plan ensures that all stakeholders, from end-users to IT support staff, are well-informed, competent in using the new system, and engaged throughout the transition process.

Training Programs for End-Users and IT Support Staff

1. **End-User Training:**
   - Develop tiered training modules catered to the different levels of user interaction with the new system, ranging from basic navigation to advanced features.
   - Utilize a combination of training delivery methods, including in-person workshops, live webinars, and self-paced online courses.
   - Create a series of quick reference guides and FAQs to support the learning process and provide a resource for post-training support.
2. **IT Support Staff Training:**
   - Offer specialized technical training for IT support staff that covers system administration, troubleshooting, and security protocols.
   - Include hands-on sessions where IT staff can practice navigating the back-end of the system and simulate resolving potential issues.
   - Provide ongoing training that aligns with system updates and emerging technologies to ensure IT staff remains proficient.

Communication Strategy to Ensure Organizational Buy-In

1. **Initial Awareness Campaign:**

- Launch an awareness campaign to introduce the organization to the upcoming changes, highlighting the benefits and improvements the new system will provide.
- Use diverse communication channels such as emails, intranet posts, newsletters, and town hall meetings to reach all employees.

2. **Ongoing Engagement:**
   - Keep the organization informed about the project's progress through regular updates.
   - Involve key stakeholders in the communication loop, including department heads and team leaders, to act as change champions within their respective areas.

3. **Leadership Endorsement:**
   - Secure visible endorsement from senior leadership to reinforce the strategic importance of the new system.
   - Encourage leaders to communicate their support through video messages, written communications, and personal involvement in training sessions.

Feedback Mechanisms to Refine User Training

1. **Post-Training Surveys:**
   - Conduct surveys immediately after training sessions to gather feedback on the effectiveness of the training, clarity of the content, and the trainer's performance.
   - Use this feedback to make real-time adjustments to the training program for subsequent sessions.

2. **Help Desk Analytics:**
   - Monitor help desk calls and support tickets to identify common issues or areas where users are struggling, indicating potential gaps in training.

- Adapt the training curriculum to address these areas and reduce the burden on the help desk.

3. **Continuous Learning and Improvement:**
   - Establish a continuous learning program that offers refresher courses, advanced training, and updates on new system features.
   - Create a user community or forum where users can share tips, best practices, and provide peer-to-peer support.

The Training and Communication Plan is designed to empower all organizational members with the knowledge and skills needed to confidently navigate the new ICAM system. By ensuring that all stakeholders understand the reasons for the change, know how to use the new system effectively, and feel supported throughout the transition, the organization can foster a positive culture around the new technology. Feedback mechanisms will serve as a vital tool for ongoing improvement, ensuring that the training programs evolve to meet the users' needs and contribute to the project's long-term success.

Testing and Quality Assurance

Testing and quality assurance are integral to the successful deployment of the mob.id and viewDS solution. This process ensures that the system is not only functional but also secure and user-friendly. A structured approach to testing will validate the integrity, performance, and usability of the new ICAM system.

Define Testing Phases and Success Criteria

1. **Unit Testing:**
   - Focus on individual components of the mob.id and viewDS systems to ensure they function correctly in isolation.

- Success Criteria: Each component should meet its specified requirements with no critical bugs.

2. **Integration Testing:**
   - Test the interaction between mob.id, viewDS, and other organizational systems to ensure seamless data exchange and functionality.
   - Success Criteria: Data flows correctly between systems, and all APIs perform as expected.

3. **System Testing:**
   - Evaluate the complete and integrated ICAM solution as a single system to ensure that it meets the overall requirements.
   - Success Criteria: The system satisfies all defined functional specifications and user stories.

4. **User Acceptance Testing (UAT):**
   - Conduct testing with actual users to ensure the system meets their needs and expectations.
   - Success Criteria: Users can complete typical tasks efficiently, and the system is approved by the user community.

Security Testing Protocols, especially for PKI-Based Access

1. **Penetration Testing:**
   - Engage external security professionals to perform penetration tests, simulating cyberattacks to identify vulnerabilities.
   - Success Criteria: The system withstands simulated attacks without breaches, and any potential vulnerabilities are addressed.

2. **PKI Infrastructure Testing:**
   - Thoroughly test the issuance, expiration, renewal, and revocation of PKI certificates and tokens.

- Success Criteria: PKI operations are secure, and certificates and tokens are managed correctly throughout their lifecycle.

3. **Identity Infrastructure Testing:**
   - Thoroughly test the issuance, expiration, renewal, and revocation of Identities and Derived Identities.
   - Success Criteria: Identity operations are secure, and identities are managed correctly throughout their lifecycle.

4. **Compliance Audits:**
   - Verify that the security measures meet relevant compliance standards (e.g., GDPR, eIDAS).
   - Success Criteria: The system passes all compliance checks with no exceptions.

Performance and Usability Testing

1. **Load Testing:**
   - Assess the system's ability to handle anticipated user loads and perform under stress.
   - Success Criteria: The system maintains responsive performance under peak load conditions.

2. **Usability Testing:**
   - Evaluate the system's interface and workflows with real users to identify any usability issues.
   - Success Criteria: Users find the system intuitive and report high satisfaction with the interface and workflows.

3. **Accessibility Testing:**
   - Ensure the system is accessible to all users, including those with disabilities, by adhering to accessibility standards (e.g., WCAG).
   - Success Criteria: The system is fully accessible, with features like screen reader compatibility and keyboard navigation fully functional.

The Testing and Quality Assurance phase is vital in delivering a secure, reliable, and user-friendly ICAM system. By establishing clear testing phases, success criteria, and rigorous security and performance testing protocols, managers can ensure that the deployed system not only meets the technical requirements but also the practical needs of end-users. This phase is the final checkpoint before the system goes live and is critical for identifying any areas that need refinement to ensure the new system's success and organizational adoption.

Deployment Plan

A well-conceived Deployment Plan ensures a smooth transition to the new ICAM system. It entails a carefully orchestrated go-live strategy, meticulous data migration, and a comprehensive plan for post-deployment monitoring and support.

Go-Live Strategy for the New ICAM System

Final Pre-Deployment Review: Conduct a final review of the entire ICAM system to ensure all components are functioning as expected and that all pre-deployment checklist items have been completed.

Communication and Coordination: Communicate the deployment schedule to all stakeholders in advance, ensuring that all parties are informed and prepared for the transition.

Establish a coordination centre to manage deployment activities and serve as the communication hub throughout the go-live process.

Phased Rollout: Implement the go-live in phases, starting with a pilot group, followed by a departmental and then a full organizational rollout. This allows for manageable increments and the ability to address issues without widespread impact.

Data Migration and System Cutover Details

Data Migration Finalization:

- Ensure that all data has been accurately migrated and validated from Active Directory to the new viewDS system before the go-live date.
- Implement a data freeze on the old system to prevent any new changes from occurring during the cutover process.

System Cutover:

- Conduct the system cutover during a period of low activity to minimize the impact on operations. This may involve temporary access restrictions or system downtime.
- Follow the detailed cutover plan that outlines every step of the process, including backups, switching over to the new system, and contingency actions if issues arise.

Post-Deployment Monitoring and Support Structure

Monitoring:

- Establish a robust monitoring system to track the performance of the new ICAM system and to quickly identify and address any operational issues.
- Monitor user activity to ensure that the new system is being used correctly and effectively.

Support:

- Set up a dedicated support team to assist users with any issues that arise post-deployment. This team should be well-versed in the new system and ready to provide immediate assistance.

- Provide additional resources such as online help documentation, support hotlines, and troubleshooting guides.

Review and Optimization:

- Schedule regular post-deployment reviews to gather user feedback, assess system performance, and identify areas for improvement.
- Use this feedback to optimize the system, making iterative enhancements to ensure the ICAM system continues to meet the organization's needs.

The Deployment Plan is the culmination of the project, transitioning the organization to the new ICAM system. By following a structured go-live strategy, ensuring a thorough data migration and cutover, and establishing a strong post-deployment monitoring and support framework, the organization can achieve a successful transition with minimal disruption to operations. This plan paves the way for a new era of identity management within the organization, one that promises enhanced security, efficiency, and user satisfaction.

Post-Implementation Review and Continuous Improvement

After the deployment of the new ICAM system, it is crucial to evaluate the implementation's success and establish a regimen for ongoing improvement. This ensures that the system not only meets initial expectations but also evolves with the organization's needs.

Schedule for Post-Implementation Review to Evaluate Project Success

Initial Review:

- Conduct an initial post-implementation review within one month of going live. This review should assess whether the project deliverables have been met and how well the new system is performing against pre-defined success metrics.
- Evaluate user satisfaction, system stability, and performance metrics.

Ongoing Evaluations:

- Set a schedule for subsequent reviews at regular intervals, such as quarterly or bi-annually, to monitor the system's long-term performance and user engagement.
- Framework for Continuous Improvement Based on User Feedback and System Performance

Feedback Collection:

Implement tools and processes to collect ongoing user feedback, such as surveys, user forums, and direct feedback mechanisms within the system itself.

Performance Analytics:

Utilize system analytics to continuously monitor performance. Pay special attention to system response times, error rates, and usage patterns to identify areas for improvement.

Improvement Initiatives:

- Establish a cross-functional team responsible for analysing feedback and performance data and initiating improvements.
- Create a process for prioritizing improvement initiatives based on their potential impact on system performance and user satisfaction.

- Long-Term Strategy for System Updates and Maintenance

Update Policy:

Develop a policy for regular system updates, including security patches, feature enhancements, and compliance adjustments. This policy should outline the process for update rollouts, including testing and user communication.

Maintenance Plan:

Create a comprehensive maintenance plan that includes regular system health checks, data backups, and recovery procedures.

Technology Roadmap:

Develop a technology roadmap to guide the future evolution of the ICAM system. This roadmap should consider emerging trends in identity management, potential integration with new technologies, and evolving security threats.

Staff Training:

Ensure that IT staff are provided with ongoing training to keep up with system updates and industry best practices.

The post-implementation review and continuous improvement phase is not the end but rather a new beginning for the ICAM system. By establishing a structured approach to evaluate and enhance the system, the organization ensures that the ICAM solution remains effective, secure, and user-friendly.

A commitment to continuous improvement reflects the organization's dedication to excellence and its adaptive response to the ever-changing landscape of digital identity management.

Conclusion

As we conclude this project plan, it's crucial to reflect on the strategic journey we've undertaken and the transformative impact anticipated from the implementation of a new Integrated Credential and Access Management (ICAM) system.

Recap of the Project's Strategic Importance and Expected Benefits

This project has been strategically designed to enhance our organizational security posture and streamline our operations through the adoption of mob.id and viewDS. By moving away from our legacy Active Directory system and embracing a robust, PKI-based ICAM solution, we expect to realize several critical benefits:

- **Strengthened Security:** The advanced security features of our new system will significantly lower the risk of data breaches and unauthorized access, safeguarding sensitive information.
- **Increased Operational Efficiency:** Automating identity and access management processes will reduce manual workload and the potential for human error.
- **Improved Compliance:** Adherence to stringent European data protection standards will be more manageable and transparent, helping us meet our legal obligations with confidence.
- **Enhanced User Experience:** Users across the organization will benefit from a more intuitive and straightforward interface, making their daily interactions with our digital environment more pleasant and productive.
- **Future-Readiness:** The new system is designed to adapt and grow with emerging technologies and evolving organizational needs, ensuring long-term sustainability.

Final Thoughts on the Significance of a Well-Implemented ICAM Solution

The successful implementation of the ICAM solution is more than just an IT upgrade—it's a strategic enabler for the organization. A well-implemented ICAM system lies at the heart of our digital transformation efforts, fostering a secure, agile, and efficient workplace. It empowers our workforce, secures our digital assets, and positions us to respond swiftly to new challenges and opportunities.

In a world where digital security and privacy are paramount, the significance of our endeavour cannot be overstated. This project marks a significant milestone in our ongoing commitment to maintaining the highest standards of security and operational excellence. By undertaking this initiative, we are not only securing our digital present but also paving the way for a more secure and innovative future. The success of this project is a testament to our organization's resilience and forward-thinking vision, and it sets a strong foundation for continued growth and success in an increasingly digital world.

This outline serves as a conceptual framework for a manager to understand the critical aspects of implementing an ICAM solution using mob.id and viewDS. It emphasizes the necessity for a secure, modern identity management system, considering the high-security demands of a large government organization. The detailed Microsoft Project plan, with specific hours and resources, would need to be developed separately, taking into account the unique aspects of the organization's environment.

Please bear in mind that while every organization is distinct, with its own set of unique challenges and characteristics, the framework provided in this plan serves merely as an exemplar— a foundational guide intended to be adapted to fit your organization's specific circumstances. For the purchasers of this book, this plan is offered as a complimentary resource, free to use and modify. It is designed to be flexible, allowing you to tailor it to meet your organization's unique requirements, and to serve as a practical instrument in implementing a robust identity management system that aligns with your operational landscape.

Appendices

Project timeline and milestones

This detailed breakdown of tasks provides a clear picture of the individual steps required in each phase of the project. It's important to note that each task may have multiple subtasks not listed here due to space constraints, and the durations given are for illustrative purposes and may need to be adjusted based on the specifics of the project at hand. This level of detail is essential for the creation of a dynamic project plan that can be adapted and managed in a project management tool like Microsoft Project

Creating a detailed project plan for transitioning from an Active Directory (AD) system to a zero-trust ICAM environment with fine-grained Attribute Based Access Control (ABAC) involves several complex stages. This plan will encompass verification against legal identities, synchronization with HR data for employment status, and establishing security clearance levels. Below is a high-level outline, broken down by phases, tasks, and key subtasks, including verification and account clean-up processes, and the implementation of strong multi-factor authentication based on location, timing, device specificity, liveness detection, and PIN codes.

A detailed project plan with durations for a complex ICAM implementation is a comprehensive task. Below is an extended version of the plan with a brief description of each task and subtask, along with estimated durations. Please note that these durations are illustrative and should be adjusted based on the specific context of the project.

Project Plan for Transition to Zero-Trust ICAM Environment

Phase 1: Project Initiation

Task 1: Project Charter Development

- **Duration**: 5 days
    - Subtask 1.1: Draft initial charter (Duration: 2 days)
        - Description: Outline the project's objectives, key deliverables, and establish high-level project milestones.
    - Subtask 1.2: Stakeholder review and finalize (Duration: 2 days)
        - Description: Review the draft with key stakeholders to incorporate feedback and gain alignment.
    - Subtask 1.3: Charter approval and dissemination (Duration: 1 day)
        - Description: Finalize and distribute the approved charter to all stakeholders for transparency and alignment.

Task 2: Stakeholder Engagement

- **Duration**: 10 days
    - Subtask 2.1: Develop stakeholder matrix (Duration: 3 days)

- Description: Identify stakeholders, assess their influence and interest, and plan engagement strategy accordingly.
- Subtask 2.2: Conduct kick-off meetings (Duration: 4 days)
  - Description: Organize and facilitate meetings with stakeholders to discuss project implications, gather initial feedback, and set expectations.
- Subtask 2.3: Establish communication plan (Duration: 3 days)
  - Description: Develop a plan that outlines how, when, and what project updates will be communicated.

Task 3: Resource Planning

- **Duration**: 7 days
  - Subtask 3.1: Define roles and assign team members (Duration: 3 days)
    - Description: Determine the project roles required and assign appropriate team members to these roles.
  - Subtask 3.2: Create budget forecast (Duration: 3 days)
    - Description: Estimate financial resources required for the project, considering personnel, software, training, and contingency costs.
  - Subtask 3.3: Setup PMO (Duration: 1 day)
    - Description: Establish a Project Management Office to centralize and coordinate project documentation, resource tracking, and budget management.

Phase 2: Requirements and Design

Task 4: Requirements Gathering

- **Duration**: 15 days
  - Subtask 4.1: IT department workshops (Duration: 5 days)
    - Description: Gather detailed technical requirements from the IT department through collaborative workshops.
  - Subtask 4.2: HR department focus groups (Duration: 5 days)
    - Description: Align employee verification processes with HR to ensure accuracy and compliance.
  - Subtask 4.3: Steering committee review (Duration: 5 days)
    - Description: Present gathered requirements to the steering committee for validation and prioritization.

Task 5: Security Clearance Structuring

- **Duration**: 10 days
  - Subtask 5.1: Define access protocols (Duration: 5 days)
    - Description: Create specific protocols for accessing data at each security clearance level in conjunction with the security team.
  - Subtask 5.2: Develop compliance checklist (Duration: 5 days)
    - Description: Prepare a checklist to ensure each security level meets audit and compliance standards.

Task 6: System Design

- **Duration**: 20 days
  - Subtask 6.1: Architecture diagram creation (Duration: 7 days)

- Description: Design a comprehensive architecture diagram for the ICAM system showing all components and integration points.
- Subtask 6.2: ABAC policy documentation (Duration: 7 days)
  - Description: Document detailed Attribute Based Access Control policies for data access at various classification levels.
- Subtask 6.3: Interface mock-ups and prototyping (Duration: 6 days)
  - Description: Develop interface mock-ups and working prototypes to visualize user interactions with the system.

Phase 3: System Development

Task 7: Identity Verification System Integration

- **Duration**: 20 days
  - Subtask 7.1: Develop API connectors (Duration: 10 days)
    - Description: Build API connectors for real-time identity verification against passport and ID card databases.
  - Subtask 7.2: HR status integration (Duration: 10 days)
    - Description: Implement a system to verify employee status against HR records before granting system access.

Task 8: Legacy System Data Synchronization

- **Duration**: 15 days
  - Subtask 8.1: Data migration ETL processes (Duration: 10 days)
    - Description: Set up Extract, Transform, Load processes for selective data migration, ensuring data integrity.
  - Subtask 8.2: Data cleansing operation (Duration: 5 days)

- Description: Perform data cleansing to eliminate outdated and redundant AD accounts, preserving necessary historical data.

Task 9: Multi-factor Authentication Setup

- **Duration**: 20 days
  - Subtask 9.1: Location and timing restrictions (Duration: 10 days)
    - Description: Implement geo-fencing and time-based restrictions for accessing the system to ensure secure operations.
  - Subtask 9.2: MDM policy configuration (Duration: 10 days)
    - Description: Configure Mobile Device Management policies to ensure only registered and verified devices can access the system.

Phase 4: Testing & Training

Task 10: Security Testing

- **Duration**: 15 days
  - Subtask 10.1: Penetration testing engagement (Duration: 10 days)
    - Description: Coordinate with external vendors to conduct thorough penetration testing, focusing on identifying any potential system vulnerabilities.
  - Subtask 10.2: ABAC enforcement validation (Duration: 5 days)
    - Description: Validate the correct enforcement of ABAC policies under various simulated scenarios to ensure system security.

Task 11: User Training Program

- **Duration**: 15 days
  - Subtask 11.1: Develop training content (Duration: 7 days)
    - Description: Create engaging training materials that are tailored to the different security clearance levels and user roles.
  - Subtask 11.2: Conduct training sessions (Duration: 8 days)
    - Description: Facilitate comprehensive training sessions for users, ensuring they are comfortable with the new system and understand the security protocols.

Phase 5: Deployment

Task 12: Pilot Deployment

- **Duration**: 10 days
  - Subtask 12.1: Select pilot group (Duration: 2 days)
    - Description: Identify and select a representative group of users from various departments to participate in the pilot program.
  - Subtask 12.2: Monitor pilot and collect feedback (Duration: 8 days)
    - Description: Closely monitor system performance and user interaction, gathering feedback for analysis and system improvement.

Task 13: Organization-wide Rollout

- **Duration**: 30 days
  - Subtask 13.1: Rollout scheduling (Duration: 5 days)
    - Description: Develop and communicate a detailed schedule for the organization-wide deployment, ensuring minimal impact on daily operations.

- Subtask 13.2: Support structure implementation (Duration: 25 days)
    - Description: Implement a robust support structure to assist users during the transition, providing immediate help for any issues encountered.

Phase 6: Post-Implementation

Task 14: Post-Deployment Review

- **Duration**: 10 days
    - Subtask 14.1: System stability and security evaluation (Duration: 5 days)
        - Description: Assess the stability and security of the ICAM system, ensuring it meets all specified requirements.
    - Subtask 14.2: User satisfaction assessment (Duration: 5 days)
        - Description: Evaluate user satisfaction with the new system, identifying any areas that require further refinement or support.

Task 15: Continuous Improvement and Maintenance

- **Duration**: Ongoing
    - Subtask 15.1: Establish routine system reviews (Duration: Ongoing)
        - Description: Set up a schedule for regular system reviews to proactively identify and address any issues, ensuring continuous system optimization.
    - Subtask 15.2: System updates and refinements (Duration: Ongoing)
        - Description: Implement a process for routine updates, security patches, and feature enhancements to keep the system aligned with

the latest industry standards and organizational needs.

This extended plan provides a more detailed overview of the tasks and subtasks required for the project. Each task should be further broken down as needed, with resources assigned, dependencies mapped, and progress meticulously tracked. This structure will serve as a solid foundation for a comprehensive, actionable project plan that can guide managers through a successful transition to a high-security, zero-trust ICAM environment.

Resource allocation and budget estimates

Certainly, let's break down the resource allocation and budget estimates for each task and subtask based on an estimated average hourly rate per role. The following table provides a high-level view of estimated hours and associated costs for the outlined project tasks:

Total Estimated Cost: To estimate the total cost, sum the "Total Cost (€)" column for all tasks and subtasks except for those with ongoing

Task	Task/Subtask Description	Role	Estimated Hours	Rate (€/hr)		Total Cost (€)
0	Project management	Project Manager	344	150	€	51.600,00
1.1	Draft initial charter	Project Manager	16	150	€	2.400,00
1.2	Stakeholder review	Project Manager	8	150	€	1.200,00
1.3	Charter approval	Project Sponsor	4	75	€	300,00
2.1	Develop stakeholder matrix	Business Analyst	24	200	€	4.800,00

2.2 Conduct kick-off meetings	Project Manager	120	150	€	18.000,00
2.3 Establish communication plan	Project Manager	28	150	€	4.200,00
3.1 Define roles	HR Manager	48	125	€	6.000,00
3.2 Create budget forecast	Financial Analyst	24	125	€	3.000,00
3.3 Setup PMO	PMO Lead	8	75	€	600,00
4.1 IT department workshops	Business Analyst	40	200	€	8.000,00
4.2 HR department focus groups	HR Specialist	40	125	€	5.000,00
4.3 Steering committee review	Project Manager	40	150	€	6.000,00
5.1 Define access protocols	Security Officer	40	150	€	6.000,00
5.2 Develop compliance checklist	Compliance Manager	40	200	€	8.000,00
6.1 Architecture diagram creation	Technical Architect	56	150	€	8.400,00
6.2 ABAC policy documentation	Security Analyst	56	100	€	5.600,00
6.3 Interface mock-ups	UX Designer	48	75	€	3.600,00
7.1 Develop API connectors	Software Developer	80	75	€	6.000,00
7.2 HR status integration	Software Developer	80	75	€	6.000,00
8.1 Data migration ETL	Data Engineer	80	75	€	6.000,00
8.2 Data cleansing operation	Data Analyst	40	75	€	3.000,00
9.1 Location and timing restrictions	Security Analyst	80	100	€	8.000,00
9.2 MDM policy configuration	IT Administrator	80	75	€	6.000,00

10.1 Penetration testing engagement	Security Consultant	80	125	€	10.000,00
10.2 ABAC enforcement validation	Security Analyst	40	100	€	4.000,00
11.1 Develop training content	Training Specialist	56	75	€	4.200,00
11.2 Conduct training sessions	Training Specialist	64	75	€	4.800,00
12.1 Select pilot group	Project Manager	16	150	€	2.400,00
12.2 Monitor pilot	Quality Assurance	64	100	€	6.400,00
13.1 Rollout scheduling	Deployment Manager	40	100	€	4.000,00
13.2 Support structure implementation	Support Manager	200	100	€	20.000,00
14.1 System stability evaluation	Quality Assurance	40	100	€	4.000,00
14.2 User satisfaction assessment	User Experience Researcher	40	75	€	3.000,00
15.1 Establish routine system reviews	Continuous Improvement Manager	Ongoing	75		Ongoing
15.2 System updates and refinements	Technical Support	Ongoing	75		Ongoing
Total investment for roll-out					
				€	**240.500,00**

www.ingramcontent.com/pod-product-compliance
Lightning Source LLC
Chambersburg PA
CBHW072157290526
45794CB00004B/1550